D1167296

"Whether we are rich or poor, the most valuable gifts we can give to our children, grandchildren and those yet to come are the treasures of our memories, our stories, our values, insights and special wisdom. Consider this book the wrapping of that gift."

—IRA BYOCK, M.D., Founder, The Missoula
Demonstration Project, and author of *Dying Well*

"Everyone wants to feel they will leave something of real value from their lives to future generations. *Ethical Wills* shows us in simple steps how to document and pass on our wisdom, experiences, life's lessons and much more to those we love. It profoundly changes and meaningfully expands the definition of an individual's legacy."

—JAMES V. GAMBONE, PH.D., author of *ReFirement:
A Boomer's Guide To Life After 50*

"Thinking through what is *really* important to each of us is a way to become more fully alive and vibrant, even while facing the fact that life does change, and eventually ends. This little manual reminds us of the obligations to be thoughtful and reflective, as well as the potential to live on in the minds and hearts of our families and friends."

—JOANNE LYNN, M.D., Director,
RAND Center to Improve Care of the Dying

"In this splendid manual, Dr. Baines blends ancient religious values with modern educational techniques. With this wisdom, all of us, from grade-schoolers to grandparents, can be guided to greater self-examination and deeper spiritual meaning."

—RABBI BARRY D. CYTRON, PH.D.

Ethical Wills

Putting your values on paper

SECOND EDITION

BARRY K. BAINES, M.D.

Da Capo
LIFE
LONG

A Member of the Perseus Books Group

Copyright © 2002, 2006 by Barry K. Baines

Healthcare Treatment Directive and Durable Power of Attorney forms (pages 192–193): Copyright © 2006 Center for Practical Bioethics, Harzfeld Building, 1111 Main Street, Suite 500, Kansas City, MO 64105-2116.

Minnesota Advance Directive form (pages 194–207): Copyright © 2005 National Hospice and Palliative Care Organization. All rights reserved. Reproduction and distribution by an organization or organized group without the written permission of the National Hospice and Palliative Care Organization is expressly forbidden.

Designed by Deborah Gayle
Set in 11-point New Caledonia

Library of Congress Cataloging-in-Publication Data

Baines, Barry K.
    Ethical wills : putting your values on paper / Barry K. Baines. — 2nd ed.
      p. cm.
    Includes bibliographical references.
    ISBN-13: 978-0-7382-1055-1 (pbk. : alk. paper)
    ISBN-10: 0-7382-1055-2 (pbk. : alk. paper) 1. Wills, Ethical. I. Title.
BJ1286.W6B35 2006
170—dc22   2006003931

First Da Capo Press printing, second edition, 2006

Published by Da Capo Press
A Member of the Perseus Books Group
http://www.dacapopress.com

Da Capo Press books are available at special discounts for bulk purchases in the U.S. by corporations, institutions, and other organizations. For more information, please contact the Special Markets Department at the Perseus Books Group, 11 Cambridge Center, Cambridge, MA 02142, or call (800) 255-1514 or (617) 252-5298, or e-mail special.markets@perseusbooks.com.

3 4 5 6 7 8 9—09 08 07 06

To my wife, Sandy, and my daughters,
Alisha and Hannah

CONTENTS

FOREWORD

In early 1999, almost five years from when I began working in the field of end-of-life care, I was sitting in a hotel room at a conference with pioneers in the field of bereavement. As we spoke about the loss of loved ones, I suddenly realized how much my father's death, when I was eighteen months old, had changed my life. I realized that, though I had often thought about my father over the years, I had spent little time understanding my loss. I began to wonder who my father really was: Was he cheery or unhappy? What books did he read? What sports did he enjoy? Above all, what values did he hold? How I would have cherished having some written communication from my father! Without such communication, I could only extrapolate partial information from the bits and pieces I had accumulated about him from my mother and others.

As a young adult, I spent some time trying to learn who my father was. Most strongly, I felt a need to learn about his views on life. My mother's explanations were cryptic, and I had no other relatives who could fill in the details. In my search I found a distant friend of my father who told me about his close friend who had known my father well. Anxiously I sought this man, but when I finally located him, I was told he had recently died. Once again I was left without detailed information about my father.

I promised myself that my own children would never suffer such an absence in their lives. When I approached age forty in 1997, I took out a blank piece of paper and began to write a note to my two sons explaining to them that if I were to die unexpectedly I wanted them to know who I was as a person and how my values had shaped our life together up until that point. I wanted them to have the direct communication from me that I had so longed for from my own father. I found the process of writing down my values and thoughts to be rather uplifting, and it made me feel that I had completed a task that was important. This little document was insufficient, but it was all I could think of at the time.

When I first met Dr. Barry Baines in 1998 and heard about ethical wills, I realized that this is what I had written to my children, without knowing that such a thing existed. I was deeply moved by Barry's work and dedication to teaching the history as well as the potential of ethical wills. This discovery connected with my unresolved sadness about the early loss of my father as well as with my satisfaction celebrating my life as a father.

It is a privilege and a personal joy for this book on ethical wills to be the first publication of The Life Institute books imprint with Perseus Publishing. The Life Institute is a non-profit educational center working with the VA Healthcare Network Upstate New York to integrate comprehensive end-of-life care as well as wellness in aging within mainstream medicine.

Throughout this book, Dr. Baines presents a clear and concise explanation of ethical wills in a positive and proactive manner. As you read this valuable work that explains ethical wills you will find that this is a book not only about creating such documents, but about living and aging well. Whenever people at any time of life take the time to examine their values, there is a great opportunity for self-examination and psychological as well as spiritual growth. Ethical wills can be a starting point for beginning to ask some age-old questions about meaning and values. As 80 million baby boomers move forward into middle age and beyond, many in our culture will begin to see aging as an opportunity to examine and record their values, sharing the process with their families. I am confident that this book on ethical wills will be a great service to many people.

Dan Tobin, M.D.
Albany, NY

INTRODUCTION TO THE SECOND EDITION

Since the publication of the first edition of *Ethical Wills: Putting Your Values on Paper,* in 2002, I have seen the interest in ethical wills spread to the estate-, legacy-, and financial-planning industries; faith communities; the healthy aging and geriatric community; and other health care–related communities.

Clearly, the public's knowledge of ethical wills is approaching the "tipping point," to use the phrase coined by Malcolm Gladwell in his bestselling book of the same name, published in 2000. I predict that over the next several years the concept of ethical wills will become as commonplace as the two better-known wills—wills of inheritance and living wills.

Why is that?

Daniel Pink, in his recent book *The Whole New Mind: Moving from the Information Age to the Conceptual Age*, writes of the marked increase in the abundance of material things over the past several decades and the meager increase in our sense of fulfillment. As a result, more people are seeking out ways to add meaning to their lives. In his book *The Real American Dream: A Meditation on Hope*, Andrew Delbanco states, "The most striking feature of contemporary culture is the unslaked craving for transcendence." The search for meaning and transcendence, and the role that an ethical will can play in meeting these needs, will continue to propel the concept into common usage.

I have been extremely gratified to see the relative ease with which individuals and groups can be guided to complete an ethical will. In addition, more and more people are taking on the responsibility to educate and assist others in this process. This is occurring in nursing homes, assisted living facilities, senior centers, adult education settings, estate-planning practices, hospice programs, and many other community venues. Clearly, this trend will continue.

When asked to write an updated introduction and additional chapter on the subject of living wills for the second edition of *Ethical Wills: Putting Your Values on Paper*, I said that I would need to think about it. My initial concern was that combining the two subjects might dilute the message about ethical wills.

Yet, in my experience over the past four years, I have found it quite common to encounter people at seminars and conferences who assumed that an ethical will must be a type of living will or will of inheritance. In addition, because I am a physician, their inclination was toward the belief that it was a living will.

I quickly realized that this was an excellent opportunity to provide information about an important and timely topic such as that of living wills while highlighting and reinforcing the complementary nature of ethical wills and living wills.

Although I believe that having a living will is important, I know that it has been an uphill battle to persuade people to write one. Only 15 percent to 18 percent of Americans have a living will. This is in spite of significant efforts by health care professionals (doctors, nurses, social workers, etc.), estate-planning professionals, and federal and state governments to encourage people to do so.

The sheer number of possible scenarios and treatment options, medical jargon, and a lack of a thorough understanding of our illnesses and treatment choices create a significant barrier to completing a living will. In addition, the questions become, will a copy be available when needed? Will it be correctly interpreted? Moreover, because we all change our minds from time to time, we may feel uncomfortable writing down detailed and specific choices for a future scenario that is hard to predict.

My hopes in writing this additional chapter on living wills are that

- You recognize the importance of choosing someone to speak on your behalf if you cannot speak for yourself
- You have a better understanding of the common medical treatments you may need to make decisions about in critical medical situations

- You realize that you can change your mind about what treatments you want to pursue
- You know that you can try a treatment for a limited time to see if you are getting the results you want
- You appreciate that having an ethical will can help your loved ones to support your decisions or to guide them in making the best decisions for you if you are unable to

The additional information included on living wills is not meant to be all-inclusive and comprehensive. Entire books have been written on this subject. You can access many resources for more information. That being said, I hope this provides a solid base of information on living wills in a way that is easy to read and understand.

Even more important, I expect that you will gain a deep appreciation of ethical wills and how they add meaning, significance, fulfillment, and peace of mind to your life and to the lives of your loved ones.

Ethical Wills

1

An Overview
of Ethical Wills

At turning points in our lives many of us ask ourselves questions of the heart and soul.

Have I fulfilled my purpose?
What will I be remembered for?
*What kind of legacy have I passed along to my family and
others?*

Thirteen years ago, I first learned about an ancient tradition for passing on personal values, beliefs, blessings, and
advice to future generations called an "ethical will." At a sub-
conscious level, I must have remembered the custom, because when my father was diagnosed with lung cancer in
1990, I asked him to write a letter about the things that he
valued. About a month before he died, my dad gave me two
handwritten pages in which he spoke about the importance

1

of being honest, getting a good education, helping people in need, and always remaining loyal to family. That letter—his ethical will—meant more to me than any material possession he could have bequeathed.

Both personally and professionally, I have become a strong proponent of the ethical will as a vehicle for clarifying and communicating the meaning in our lives to our families and communities. I strongly believe that those who wish to reflect on and share life's experience will find an ethical will a useful tool. Those who wish to examine their moral underpinnings discover it to be an excellent forum for contemplation. Those who want to be remembered authentically and for their gifts of heart, mind, and spirit take satisfaction in knowing what they hold most valued is "on the record," not to be lost or forgotten.

As a family-practice specialist for more than two decades and a hospice physician for the past fourteen years, caring for patients who are terminally ill, I've seen many people struggle to come to terms with the lives they've led. In 1998, in collaboration with one of our hospice program chaplains, I introduced the concept of writing an ethical will. Since then, a number of patients successfully created a document. However, due to personal circumstance or the urgency of time, some found it just too difficult an undertaking.

To make it easier for everyone, I developed a *"how to"* booklet, *The Ethical Will Resource Kit*, containing step-by-step instructions and exercises. This hands-on guide has helped more than 3,000 people in all stages of life to contemplate and write an ethical will. *Ethical Wills* expands on many subjects found in *The Ethical Will Resource Kit,* including the history of ethical wills; reasons for creating (and, if needed, periodically updating) the document; the many and varied uses of an ethical will; and preservation and presentation options. It also contains a number of new exercises and approaches to development, gleaned from training diverse groups and from exchanging ideas with visitors to my Web site, www.ethicalwill.com.

My workshop experience has taught me that there are different stages of readiness that people go through in creating an ethical will. I describe the stages below along with guidance as to which chapters of *Ethical Wills* might be of most benefit to you.

The Education stage: At this stage, the concept of ethical wills may be new to you. However, the idea of creating a legacy beyond your worldly possessions is something you've thought of before. You'd like to learn more about creating a personal legacy and about ethical wills.

Start with Chapter 2. You will gain a good overview of what ethical wills are all about and a sense of their history. You may want to look at a few of the ethical will examples in Appendix I. If you're still interested, you're probably moving on to the next stage.

The Willingness stage: The idea of creating a legacy appeals to you. You'd like to figure out your personal reasons for moving ahead.

Start with Chapter 2 if you'd like more background information on ethical wills. Or, begin with Chapter 3, which helps you identify the reasons you're writing an ethical will. Read some examples of ethical wills in Appendix I, as well, especially those written by people that you can identify with. At this point, you may be ready to make a commitment to move on to the next stage. If not, consider checking out the ethical will Web site and signing up for the "Ethicalwill.com Newsletter." Being exposed to the idea over time may help you to move on to the preparation stage. Think about reading some of the recommended books listed in Appendix II.

The Preparation stage: Determine the most comfortable approach for creating your ethical will.

If you're preparing to write your ethical will, Chapter 4 is where you want to go. You'll be able to examine the different approaches you can use for writing an ethical will and decide which one is best. As in the previous stage, if you feel like you're getting stuck, read (or reread) Chapters 2 and 3. You may also want to look at some of the other resources and references in Appendix II that can help you in this preparatory stage.

The Action stage: You've selected your approach and have begun the actual work of creating your ethical will.

Chapter 4 will provide you with a range of approaches to choose from. You are already working on one or several exercises. If you prefer "having company" while writing your ethical will, check out the ethical will Web site for class listings in your neighborhood, or consider contacting local clergy or other community organizations to see if they are interested in sponsoring a workshop on ethical wills. Or, create your own community of interested people to work on this activity.

The Completion stage: You've now completed your ethical will. Chapter 5 focuses on physical preservation of your ethical will and ideas for sharing the will with your family and community.

The Review/Renewal stage: You're considering how and when to update or review your ethical will. Concentrate on Chapter 5; this section presents ideas on the review and renewal of your ethical will.

Exactly how you use this book will depend on your own starting point, sticking points, and other points along the road to completion. It's not uncommon to move back and forth between stages of readiness. Of course, I hope that you'll decide to read the entire book.

As you put pen to paper or fingertips to keyboard, remember that every ethical will is as unique as the person writing it. I trust you'll enjoy the creation process and be pleased with the outcome.

2

An Ancient Custom
Moves Forward

A Personal Experience

I remember the phone call I received from Dr. Stanley that cold January day in 1990. I had returned to Minnesota several weeks earlier, after our yearly family excursion to Florida to visit my parents. Dad was feeling a bit tired, and I noticed he couldn't play as many sets of tennis as he wanted. He also had a cough that didn't want to go away.

"My son the doctor, what should I do?" he said.

"Go see Dr. Stanley," I replied.

He did. "Walking pneumonia" was the diagnosis. When it didn't improve with antibiotics, Dr. Stanley suggested a bronchoscopy. This calls for a small fiber-optic tube to be inserted into the bronchial tubes, allowing the doctor to make a better diagnosis. A tumor was discovered and a biopsy was taken. It was lung cancer. The prognosis wasn't good.

Two weeks later, back in Florida, I asked my dad two questions. "Is there anything you haven't done that you'd like to do while you still are feeling O.K.?"

"Just to have another fifteen or twenty years of retirement," he said jokingly.

"At some point, would you write a letter that talks about things that have been important to you in your life?" I asked, not even knowing why I wanted that from him.

A strange request, he thought. Dad was never much of a letter writer. He said he'd think about it.

Eight months passed. A few weeks before he died, my father sent the letter I had asked for. Poignant memories of him come flooding back whenever I read it. I share it with you with pride, awe, and gratitude. I later discovered that before he died, he decided to write "good-bye letters" to my brother, several beloved nieces and nephews, and his older brother.

Dear Barry and Sandy:

A few words to express my feelings and thoughts while time is running out on me. Some standard values I have lived by throughout my life are that I have always believed in honesty and advocated truthfulness.

I cherish the family with all my heart. I always felt I gave of myself to each of you. The satisfaction and gratification I received in return is in the accomplishments of my children. No father could be as proud as your father is of you. You have more than exceeded my greatest expectations. You continue to move forward in a manner that makes me love you more and more. I'm proud to say, "that's my son!"

Through the years, I've tried to take care of my family and provide some of the better things in life. I tried and succeeded in being able to give my children a good education. Although I was only a working man, many were the times I worked two jobs for the extra money so the family could have a little bit more. I had often thought of going into some kind of business, but didn't have the expertise in any particular field, or the finances to afford the luxury of risk. I'm proud to say that you have shown me through the years, the aggressiveness that I lacked emerged in you.

I have tried to be financially sound and leave behind an adequate amount of finances to carry your mother through the rest of her days. Since no one can predict the future, I ask that should it ever be necessary, see that your mother remains comfortable financially and otherwise.

Sandy, you have always made me proud with your accomplishments and different endeavors. You have never undertaken a task that was under-achieved. Through the years you have been in my confidence and as close as a daughter. You are a good wife and excellent mother. Barry could not have picked a finer mate.

My concentration is not too great at this point, as I'm sure I can say much more.

I hope [your daughters] Alisha and Hannah follow in the
footsteps of the family. I love you all.
Dad

WHAT ARE ETHICAL WILLS AND WHERE DID THEY COME FROM?

Ethical Wills and Their Origins

Give every man thy ear, but few thy voice,
Take each man's censure, but reserve thy judgement . . .
Neither a borrower nor a lender (be),
For (loan) oft loses both itself and friend . . .
This above all: to thine own self be true,
and it must follow, as the night the day,
Thou canst not then be false to any man.

—Polonius to his son, Laertes
from *The Tragedy of Hamlet, Prince of Denmark*,
William Shakespeare

No, the most famous bard of the Western world did not invent the ethical will. He simply borrowed the convention to move his characters' story forward.

Dating back to biblical times, elders and leaders offered prayers and proffered advice of an ethical nature to family members and disciples, bidding them to go forward and lead full, principled, and virtuous lives. The Hebrew Bible contained the first tracings of ethical wills, although evidence of this concept may be found in early religious and spiritual teachings in other cultures. Genesis, chapter forty-nine in the Hebrew Bible recounts Jacob gathering his twelve sons around his deathbed. He reserves his most loving blessings for his son Joseph, saying:

> *Even by the God of thy father, who shall help thee,*
> *And by the Almighty, who shall bless thee,*
> *With blessings of heaven above,*
> *Blessings of the deep that coucheth beneath,*
> *Blessing of the breasts, and of the womb.*
> *The blessings of thy father*
> *Are mighty beyond the blessings of my progenitors*
> *Unto the utmost bound of the everlasting hills;*
> *They shall be on the head of Joseph,*
> *And on the crown of the head of the prince among his brethren.*

Another example is found in Moses' farewell to the Children of Israel (Deuteronomy 33). After forty years wandering through the desert and on the verge of entering the Promised Land, Moses is told by God that he will not be allowed to enter the Promised Land. Like a father laying his hands from a deathbed on the heads of his children, the departing Leader walks through the camp blessing the individual

11

tribes of Israel as he passes along. Then, as he walks up the mountain to meet his destiny, he stops and turns to behold the whole multitude for the last time. And, lifting up his hands, Moses pronounces a final benediction on the people of Israel.

The Book of Proverbs is also a rich source of moral tidings. Usually manifest in the form of instructions from father to son, these ethical wills strive to impart life lessons and faith-based values, and appear to have been written for a generation grown distant from its religious roots.

The Christian Bible contains numerous illustrations of the ethical will custom as well. John 15–17 recounts Jesus' parting blessings and advice to his loyal followers:

If you abide in me, and my words abide in you,
    ask for whatever you wish, and it will be done for you.
    My Father is glorified by this, that you bear much fruit
    and become my disciples . . .
    I have said these things to you so that your joy may be complete.
    This is my commandment, that you love one another as I have loved you.
    No one has greater love than this, to lay down one's life for one's friends.
    You are my friends if you do what I command you . . .
    I am giving you these commands so that you may love one another.

In each of these instances, the ethical will was transmitted orally, only later to be recorded by religious scholars preparing the first collection of narrative and normative writings that would form the basis for sections of the Hebrew and Christian Bibles.

Contents of ethical wills have evolved over time. In scriptural writings these treatises generally reflect future blessings, moral directives, and burial instructions. From the twelfth to the fourteenth centuries, ethical wills grew to include ethical values and beliefs of the writer and to impart information of a personal historical nature. Ethical wills also began to appear as attachments to legal wills, delivered, of course, after the death of the author.

In ancient times, most people had little opportunity to control the distribution of their property (assuming they owned any at all); however, they were free to speak their minds as it related to the disposition of "moral" assets. Ethical wills were particularly advantageous outlets for women, since society's rules usually precluded them from writing a legal will or dispensing property as they wished. Historians have found examples of ethical wills authored by women during the medieval period, usually in the form of letters or books written to their children.

The use of ethical wills seemed to have tapered off during the latter half of the first millennium, at least in Western cultures. However, the decline has reversed itself over the past several decades. Public awareness of the custom has grown, as current generations take increasing interest in activities that contribute meaning and purpose to our lives. As baby boomers and their parents grow older, their desire to preserve and bequeath a legacy of values will continue to increase.

Often I'm asked why these documents are called ethical wills. Although the term is of uncertain origin, I have some opinions about this label. As writing became more common, attachments to legal wills were discovered that contained the title of "Teachings of the Fathers." While legal wills provided instructions on what to do with material assets, the "ethical" sections contained instructions on how to lead a moral and upright life. I like the analogy: Legal wills bequeath *valuables*, while ethical wills bequeath *values*.

Another important issue to consider is the legality of the documents. Although a "last will and testament" and living wills are considered legal documents under the law, ethical wills are not. This has caused some controversy within the legal community as it relates to incorporating the use of ethical wills in estate planning.

People usually associate the term "will" with "after death." Legal wills are read after death. At one time ethical wills were passed on and read after death as well; however, that's less often the case today. A living will, a document that contains specific instructions about medically related issues, is meant to be followed while the person is still alive but unable to communicate his or her wishes directly at the time these decision points are reached.

What all three types of wills have in common is the fact that they provide instructions to others as to the intentions of the author.

Though it's unclear as to the exact origin and rationale for using the term "ethical will," I choose to respect and honor their 3,000-year-old history. Thus, I continue to use the term "ethical will," and I usually follow it with an explanation. To me, it represents continuity through the generations.

This is a good time to introduce an exercise titled "Linking the Generations." As you think about what you might include in your own ethical will, you need to realize that there will be contributions from your past, present, and future. Some of our values and beliefs have been passed on to us from our predecessors. Our own life experiences shape our character and help form a foundation of our values and principles. Looking into the future, ponder what we might yet become and what we have left to do. This exercise will help you create content for your ethical will in at least a couple of ways. First, it will highlight your role as a link between past and future generations. Second, it's likely to evoke memories of important events in your life, and stir your thinking about what you might include in your ethical will.

Get a few sheets of paper and a pencil or pen, and you're ready to begin. When you've finished the exercise, save what you've written for later.

Exercise: Linking the Generations

1. Write down the name of a deceased relative whom you may have been named after, or whom you may have heard stories or "legends" about when you were growing up.
2. Imagine going back in time to talk to that person. What questions would you ask them? What would you want to know about their lives? Ask them how they want to be remembered.
3. With today as your starting point, "fast forward" 50–100 years. Imagine one of your future family or community members doing this same exercise and selecting you. Reflect on what you've written here. I think you'll see that the link between the past and the future will produce some wonderful contents for your ethical will. Many things that we consider "ordinary" or not very interesting in our day-to-day life will be quite riveting 50–100 years from now.

WHAT'S IN AN ETHICAL WILL?

As Forrest Gump said, in the movie with the same name, "Life is like a box of chocolates. You never know what you're gonna get." Like a box of chocolates, the contents of ethical wills can vary. On the other hand, you typically find *chocolate* in a box of chocolates. Let's review themes commonly found in an ethical will. Authors reflect on their past, take stock of who they are in the present, and project into the future with their hopes, wishes, and requests.

Common themes from our past:

- Meaningful personal or family stories
- Lessons learned from personal or familial experience
- Regrets

Common themes from the present:

- Personal values and beliefs
- Values and beliefs of the author's faith community
- Expressions of love and gratitude
- Apologies

Common themes for the future:

- Blessings, dreams, and hopes for present and future generations
- Advice and guidance
- Requests
- Funeral plans

Additional themes appear in the authentic ethical wills that comprise Appendix I.

If there are certain themes that resonate with you, jot them down on a piece of paper as a placeholder for inclusion in the ethical will you wish to create.

Now that you know what ethical wills are, where they originated, and how they were used in the ancient world, we can move into our own time to see when they are being written, and why they've become so popular as a tool to provide meaning in our lives.

Why and When to
Write an Ethical Will

If you're starting on this chapter, or have completed Chapter 2, you've probably graduated from the "Education" stage of readiness and are ready to move into the next stage of creating your ethical will—the Willingness stage!

At this stage, if you recall, the idea of creating a personal legacy appeals to you. You'd like to figure out your personal reasons for moving ahead and to identify some specific reasons for writing your ethical will.

This chapter details why we write an ethical will, and to understand when to consider writing one.

DISCOVERING YOUR REASONS

People choose to write ethical wills for a variety of reasons (I've compiled a list of them cited by participants in workshops and seminars I've conducted over the past few years). Whatever the motivation, by now you know that ethical wills come from the heart.

In the same way that every ethical will is unique, your motivation to write one will be unique as well. Sometimes, it's helpful to review what others say about why they chose to write an ethical will. Several of these reasons may resonate or "speak" to you or to your situation. Or, these items may stimulate your own thinking to help you identify your core reasons.

Creating an ethical will is a way to:

- learn about myself
- reflect on my life
- affirm myself
- affirm what others mean to me
- articulate what I stand for
- tell stories that illustrate my values
- tell stories for perpetuity

An ethical will is a forum in which to:

- fill in knowledge gaps of will recipients by providing historic or ancestral information that links generations
- convey feelings, thoughts, and "truths" that are hard to say face-to-face
- express regrets and apologies

- open the door to forgiving and being forgiven
- come to terms with my mortality

Writing an ethical will may be:

- a spiritual experience that provides a sense of completion to my life
- a loving undertaking that helps my loved ones "let go" when my time comes

Having reviewed the above list, and with your newfound knowledge about this custom, take your pad or paper and spend a few minutes jotting down your thoughts as to why you want to create an ethical will.

LIFE TRANSITIONS AND LIFE-CHANGING EVENTS

Elaine Ellis-Stone from St. Paul, Minnesota, wrote this while she was pregnant with her first child:

> [I know] ethical wills traditionally are written in retrospect. A parent may reflect back over . . . life, picking out the most important lessons learned to pass on to his or her family. I see my ethical will more as a work-in-progress. I hope to update it as our child grows and reaches other milestones in life.

When is a *good* time to write an ethical will? There are at least two responses to this question: (1) at turning points in your life; (2) when an event or situation encountered is cause for serious reflection. The fact that you're reading this book is probably an indication that you or someone close to you is or soon will be in one of these *places*.

Whenever you decide to write an ethical will is the "right" time. However, an important driver may be the level of urgency you feel to do this.

Specific events and experiences in life are unique to each individual. However, our experiences as human beings clearly have a lot in common, and may be grouped into transitional life stages. Transitional times are often stressful for us, yet, they can also be times of reflection. For example, the change of status from single to married, starting and raising a family, becoming an "empty nester," and becoming a grandparent are all passages many of us traverse. Creating an ethical will at any and all such junctures can be of significant value to writer and reader(s) alike.

Let's look at some examples.

Transitions

- Single Adults:
  Several years ago, flying home from a conference, I struck up a conversation with the person seated next

to me. As often happens in my encounters, the discussion turned to ethical wills. My seatmate, an architect in her late thirties who didn't plan to marry or have children, was taken with the concept. She could see the value of creating an ethical will for her family of friends, and also for her extended family of aunts, uncles, and cousins as a way to fill gaps in her genealogical tree. She planned to create an ethical will as an attachment to her legal will setting up a charitable fund for her church and Habitat for Humanity, the institutions to which she is most devoted. Either approach would bequeath her values, which she feels are beneficial to future generations of her loved ones and society at large.

• Betrothed Couples:

A soon-to-be-married couple was encouraged by their clergyman to articulate and share with one another their personal values and principles to live by. Each created an ethical will focused on those areas. Now, as husband and wife, the two use the information as a basis for mutual understanding.

On a lighter note, from my personal experience, I know I could have bypassed a number of spats with my spouse, Sandy, had I known before we were married that when it came to storing leftovers, she was "Lady Reynolds Wrap™" (an aluminum foil user), while I was the "Saran™-man" (a plastic wrap user). Didn't she know when you use aluminum foil you can't see what's in a food container? Isn't it common knowledge that covering perishable items with aluminum foil will turn your refrigerator into a mold-growing laboratory in no time? Penicillin has already been invented! On the other hand, I don't like being accused of depleting the country's petroleum reserves to manufacture a product that can't easily be recycled or reused.

The good news is that we've reconciled these differences by using containers to store food that are made of glass (so you can see what's inside) with an opaque cover that can be used over and over again!

Of course, I'm not suggesting that how you store leftovers is an important value to be transmitted to future generations. This example was just meant to highlight how apparently superficial differences (using aluminum foil vs. plastic wrap) can reveal underlying values (environmental concerns, avoiding waste, frugality).

- Birth of a Child:

   The birth of a child is another opportune time to take pause and reflect on what is important to each spouse, as together they embark on the challenging journey of parenthood. The husband and wife who were expecting their first child thought ahead. Combined, their ethical wills helped create a joint framework for child rearing. Imagine the disputes these two avoided by discussing potential conflict areas up front!

- Growing Families and Children:

    Ethical wills can also be used to state family values clearly and may result in improving communication between parents and children. I recall sharing the contents of my ethical will with my daughters, then still in their teenage years. They appreciated receiving it. Although they were not surprised by what I had written, the girls were quick to point out, in a good-natured way, that they would be more aware of making sure I acted consistently on things I wrote were important to me, such as family vacations.

    Ethical wills have been created by those as young as preteens. A patient of one of my partners was only ten years old when he developed brain cancer. As treatments grew less helpful and he approached death, the boy expressed to his parents how strongly he believed in the importance of preserving the environment. This declaration was his ethical will. Honoring the child's wishes, his family set up a community-based environmental initiative that later received national attention. The project continues today.

- Separation and Divorce:

    Just as an ethical will may be of assistance when people come together, it has the potential to be of use when they move apart. Some family counselors routinely encourage divorced (especially noncustodial) parents to create ethical wills. For children of divorce the document may offer a measure of security at an insecure time by reaffirming the values to which their parents aspire. In turn, writing an ethical will may provide needed solace to parents who feel the need to reassure uneasy children that they will continue to uphold their parental role.

Several of the ethical wills presented in Appendix I relate directly to themes of divorce, decisions about custody, and reassurances that the noncustodial parent will "be there" for their child when needed.

- Middle Age and Beyond:

  The latter half of our lives is one of the most valuable times to create an ethical will. It is a period of great opportunity to harvest our life experiences, convert them into wisdom, and fulfill the responsibility of passing on what we have learned on to future generations, to our families, communities, or both. The baby boomer generation is gaining an awareness of their personal yearning to find, express, and pass on the meaning and purpose in their lives, as well as to capture the stories, values, and meaning of their aging parents.

- End of Life:

  As we approach the inevitable end of our lives, writing an ethical will adds a transcendent dimension to our presence on this planet by providing a link to future generations. It is a way to transform values and beliefs into a legacy, which may well be accompanied by a profound sense of satisfaction, completion, and continuation, all at the same time.

WHEN EVENTS CHANGE YOUR LIFE

Going through challenging life experiences can be a catalyst for creating an ethical will. Again, what is viewed as a challenge is unique to each individual; however, there are common refrains. Below are responses I've heard most often from workshop participants.

Life-changing events that provide the impetus to create an ethical will include:

- experiencing the death of a loved one
- facing surgery
- being diagnosed with a serious illness
- losing a job
- getting a divorce
- the birth of, or marriage of, a child or grandchild

A case in point, as told to me by a friend:

It was December when I fit an MRI into an annual shopping outing. Neither the neurologist nor I expected it to explain my infrequent dizzy spells. When I returned home, I had a message to call the physician at home—an ominous request.

He told me I had a walnut-sized tumor pressing on my brain stem. Although not likely malignant, it still had to come out.

I had two weeks to put my life in order, including filing some overdue legal documents, tying up loose ends at work, and keeping Christmas for my family. Although tasks kept me busy in the daytime, my nights were consumed with fear.

Informed consent for the surgery included all that could happen: paralysis, loss of speech and the ability to swallow, blindness, deafness, facial deformity, or death. I made peace with the potential disabilities by rationalizing I'd deal with that when it happened. Death was another matter. I was a forty-five-year-old single mother of two teenagers. How could I leave my children?

In the hospital the night before surgery, after saying good-bye to my children and visitors, I lay awake thinking of my children and their futures. I felt compelled to write "only if" letters. My available stationery was a school notebook. I borrowed two envelopes from a nurse. Writing the letters left me unexpectedly peaceful, a serenity that was still there in the morning when I was wheeled off to surgery. With gratitude I can report I survived. After a few brief weeks of rehabilitation I returned home from the hospital. I never delivered these letters. A number of years later, while rummaging through some boxes, my children inadvertently came across my "only if" letters and asked to read them. Our relationship is all the richer as a result.

(These "only if" letters can be found in Appendix I.)

✿　　✿　　✿

This might be a good time for you to take a few moments to gauge your level of urgency to create an ethical will. Are you going through a transitional life stage at this time? Are you facing a challenging life situation? These are the concerns that help you understand your personal urgency to undertake this task.

If you're able to identify these drivers, the next chapter will provide you with practical approaches for how to create your ethical will.

How to Write an Ethical Will

THREE APPROACHES FOR WRITING YOUR ETHICAL WILL

At this point, you have an understanding of what an ethical will is, and what you can expect to find in one. Additionally, you probably have a good grasp on why you want to write one and when would be a good time to do this. If this describes you, you're transitioning into the next two stages of readiness, the Preparation stage and the Action stage.

If you don't think you're ready for the Preparation stage and you need more time to think about and process the concept, access some of the suggested resources listed at the end of the book. Try to engage your friends and family in conversations about ethical wills. Don't be surprised if others express an interest in creating their own ethical will, too.

In the Preparation stage, you'll want to review different ways to move toward your goal of creating your ethical will. This chapter presents three approaches arranged in order from "easiest" to "hardest," according to:

- your available time (little time to lots of time)
- your sense of urgency (high to low urgency)
- your comfort with writing in general (very structured to very open-ended)

Once you select the approach that's most comfortable for you, you'll find ample information to move ahead confidently. Each approach follows a similar strategy by first collecting key ideas and elements, then organizing the information to be integrated into your document later. You can use any or all of them.

Another option is to work with others who are also interested in writing an ethical will. Check with local community organizations to see if they offer any group classes on this subject. Or, try to set up your own community of people interested in writing ethical wills. You can do this by using bulletin boards or contacting your community's religious, educational, social services, and seniors' services organizations. It's often easier to create an ethical will in a community setting. Sharing your ideas and listening to the ideas of others will stimulate your thinking and help you come up with additional content. It also is mutually motivating.

Regardless of which approach or method you choose to begin working on your ethical will, you have progressed into the Action stage.

Here's a quick overview of the three approaches.

Approach #1
Starting with an Outline and a List of
Items to Choose From

- The easiest approach for getting started
- The best approach for those who want to produce a document quickly
- Features a complete outline structure and several item choices in each category of the outline

Approach #2
Starting with an Outline and Specific
Writing Exercises

A good method to use if you want to:

- create some detailed material in a short time
- establish some momentum right away
- have natural "next steps" for building on and revising your draft if you started with approach #1

Approach #3
Starting with a Blank Sheet of Paper

A good approach for you if:

- a blank sheet of paper feels like an opportunity
- you prefer a more open-ended approach
- you already keep a journal or a diary

Now that you have an overall picture of the different approaches, let's get started on the actual exercises.

APPROACH #1
STARTING WITH AN OUTLINE AND
A LIST OF ITEMS TO CHOOSE FROM

This exercise will provide you with a framework to quickly and efficiently complete a rough draft. Then you can edit the phrases and sentences you chose, so that they'll be more reflective of your writing style and your own thinking. Seeing these phrases will stimulate other ideas and thoughts you will want to write about.

Ethical wills have many elements in common. Here they are consolidated and arranged in a combination of the more common phrases and frequent theme categories. The uniqueness of your ethical will is in the stories that fill in the pictures that this framework provides.

This "master template" guarantees that you will have a first draft of an ethical will. You can personalize it further by adding your life stories and experiences that make it the only one of its kind. Approaches #2 and #3 can help you to revise and enrich your draft.

As you explore the different categories and items in the following pages, have a pad of paper ready to write down your selections. Choose as many of the items as you want to. As you write them down, you can revise them by changing the wording of the phrases or adding to them.

Opening Thoughts

- To my unborn child: I am writing this in eager anticipation of your birth. I know that I have much to learn about being a parent . . .
- Dear family and friends: I leave to you these things that I have learned through my life . . .
- Dear children: A few words to express my thoughts and feelings about what is important to me . . .
- To my family: In reading my ethical will, I hope you find few surprises because . . .
- I want you to know how important you are in my life and how much I love you . . .

If you wish, write down your own opening thoughts.

Now that you've started your ethical will, you can begin to move on to identify the things you value and stand for. The following subcategories under "Values and Beliefs" are arranged in a way that reflects the level of frequency that these themes appear in ethical wills. Concentrate on the ones that seem most important to you.

VALUES AND BELIEFS

The Importance of Family and Other Relationships

- As I've grown older I continue to value the family more and more. . . .
- So much of what I am is because of Grandpa, and I dearly miss him every day. . . .
- I had a special relationship with my grandmother. From her I learned that one should "do good for the sake of good, not for the sake of reward. . . ."
- I hope, especially for my family, to get along in life. . . .
- If you find a good, true friend, hold on to him or her as hard as you can. . . .

If you wish, write down your own ideas about family and other relationships.

Religion/Spirituality

- I hope you continue the traditions and faith of (fill in your faith community) and pass these on to future generations. . . .

- My mission is to serve God by creating a balance between family, friends, profession, and community. . . .
- I know I have never offered much in the way of spiritual guidance. However, I hope that my manner of living has served as a living example of my own moral code. . . .
- Faith in God is important. I am not all that religious, but I am a believer. . . .
- (Fill in your faith community) is your foundation but it is also important to be part of the larger world. . . .

If you wish, write down your own thoughts about religion and spirituality.

The Importance of Education/Learning/Knowledge

- An important value to cherish is that as long as you live you can continue to learn. . . .
- It is a privilege and responsibility to share your knowledge and your love of learning with others. . . .
- Read as if your life depended on it; it does. . . .
- I tried to give you, my children, a good education. . . .
- Have a passion for learning. Learn for the sake of learning and not with an eye only to a future career or how much money you can make. . . .

Record your own thoughts about the importance of education, learning, and knowledge.

Here's one example of how you can select a phrase and then enrich it with a personal anecdote. In the above category, one of the phrases is: *"I tried to give you, my children, a good education."* The story is as follows:

> Providing a good education was important to me because of what I experienced growing up. I was in the tenth grade during the Great Depression in the 1930s. I had to leave school in order to go to work. Many of my friends did the same thing. I never felt I had the chance to get a good education. I made a promise to myself that when I raised a family, my kids would go to college and hopefully beyond. You can always earn a living with your back. It's better to earn a living with your head.

Respect for Life

- Respect life—yours and others. Treat other people the way you want to be treated. . . .
- Be positive and look for the good in people. . . .
- What is hateful to you do not do unto others. . . .
- Cultivate a diverse group of friends and remember to judge a person as an individual, not by their ethnic, religious, or racial group. . . .

If you wish, write down your own ideas about respect for life.

Learning from Mistakes

- Learn from mistakes. It's impossible to be successful in everything you try to do. . . .

- Don't be afraid of making mistakes. Just be sure you learn something from them. . . .
- You can learn more from a mistake than from always doing everything right. . . .
- Don't fear mistakes, for mistakes are the springboard of future success. . . .
- If you focus on things that are important to you, failures may come, but they will be fewer. . . .

If you wish, write down your own thoughts about learning from mistakes.

Being Honest, Truthful, and Sincere

- Be sincere yet decisive. . . .
- Act as if all your actions will be part of a story published in the newspapers. . . .
- I have always believed in honesty and advocated truthfulness. . . .
- Be sincere and honest and learn to recognize these qualities in others. Call these people your friends.

If you wish, write down your own thoughts about being honest, truthful, and sincere.

Giving and Receiving

- In giving you make your life worthwhile. . . .
- If you don't take, you will have nothing to give. . . .
- Don't refuse to accept: Others need a chance to give also. . . .
- In sharing, one learns, experiences, and reaps the highest level of satisfaction. . . .

If you wish, write down your ideas on giving and receiving.

Good and Evil

- Do good and avoid evil. . . .
- Be aware of the evils of the world, but do not be consumed by them. . . .
- I hope you will make the world a better place, both on a smaller scale and in the wider sense. . . .

If you wish, jot down your thoughts on the value of doing good.

The Importance of Humor

- Having a good sense of humor is very important. . . .
- Humor can help you to get through difficult situations. . . .
- Humor ought to be a large part of every person's day. . . .

If you wish, jot down your ideas about the value of humor.

LESSONS AND REFLECTIONS ABOUT LIFE

Lessons

- Act on situations and opportunities, rather than be acted upon. . . .
- Don't make assumptions of what people need. Ask them. . . .

- Have a willingness to be open. You will learn more by listening than by speaking. . . .
- Learn to be humble. . . .
- Hard work and a broad understanding will bring success. . . .

If these phrases stimulate your own thoughts about life lessons, jot them down.

Reflections

- Remember that one person can make a difference. . . .
- Stay true to yourself and give your best effort. . . .
- Be courageous and persistent and accept differences. . . .
- If you gauge your achievements on those of others, you will most likely be disappointed. . . .
- Don't let yourselves be easily discouraged. . . .

Record your own reflections.

Hopes for the Future

- I hope that you can remember the good memories. . . .
- I hope you are as lucky as I was in finding a soulmate like (name) to share your life with. . . .
- Pursue your chosen path, study things that interest you, and use your college education to get you started. . . .
- Try to be a part of the solution, not part of the problem. . . .
- Keep before you for inspiration a vision of the way things ought to be, and help us move, albeit so slightly, in that direction. . . .

If you wish, write down additional hopes for the future.

Love

- My love for my grandchildren is too great to express in words. I hope I have expressed it in other ways. . . .
- Show everyone you love that you love him or her, and be sure to tell him or her as well. . . .
- Be generous with love. . . .
- To my precious family, I express my deep, unyielding love, for they were a great part of my life. . . .
- No matter how lost or disconsolate you may seem at various points in your life, I hope this helps to bring you back on track: that your parents loved you intensely, unconditionally, and imaginatively. . . .

If you want to record your own thoughts about love, jot them down.

Forgiveness

- I apologize for the times I wasn't the mom you would have liked. . . .
- Never be afraid to say, "I'm sorry, please forgive me. . . .
- Forgive whatever misunderstandings there are. . . .
- Forgive me if I have hurt you in any way or if I have been too hard on you at times. . . .

If you think of more ways to express forgiveness, record them on your writing pad.

Requests

- Because no one can predict the future, I ask that should it ever be necessary, please see that your mother remains comfortable financially and otherwise. . . .
- Enrich your mind, exercise your body, and feed your spirit with music, art, meaningful work, friends, and helping the community at large. . . .

- Be broad-minded and curious about the world. . . .
- Try to find joy and beauty in the simple, ordinary things that life has to offer. . . .
- Time is precious; do not waste it or take it for granted. . . .

If you think of additional ideas for your own requests, add them to your draft.

Concluding Thoughts

- You all have been a great source of joy and strength for me. I love you all very much. . . .
- Finally, I am thankful for all those who have been good to me and have been helpful. I've learned to live a good life. I hope a good life for all. Good-bye. . . .
- As I close here, I have to chuckle because I realize that even at the end of my life I do not stop giving directions. Humor me, it is who I am. . . .
- My love will always be with you—you get to keep it and remember it forever. . . .
- I love you all. . . .

If you wish, write your own concluding thoughts.

APPROACH #2
STARTING WITH AN OUTLINE AND
SPECIFIC WRITING EXERCISES

In this section you'll find specific writing exercises with illustrations of how these exercises might look when completed. Plan on completing several or all of the exercises over a period of weeks rather than trying to finish them in one sitting.

You will want to think about some of the ideas presented, so take your time.

After you have a working draft, you can move categories around so they are in an order that makes sense to you. You can add more categories using the outline in approach #1.

Another way to use this approach is to ask a family member or friend to help. Present your thoughts and stories verbally. Your helper can tape-record your discussions or take notes to create a written transcript. You might want someone to interview you with specific questions to stimulate your thoughts and memories. These techniques can serve as a sounding board and offer feedback. An added advantage is that hearing what you've said rather than reading it may help you determine whether the words you've chosen convey what you intend.

Use separate sheets of paper for each outline section, or buy a blank notebook to write in. Consider the following as a high-level outline structure for your ethical will:

1. opening thoughts
2. statements of values and beliefs
3. meaningful and personally instructive life experiences
4. hopes for the future
5. concluding thoughts

It's sometimes easiest to get started on writing if you have the salutation already in place. Use any of these for starters, or just use one as a placeholder.

Possible openings for your ethical will:

- To my family:
- To my dearest family:
- Dear . . . (use actual names of the recipients of your ethical will):
- To the people who are most important to me:

You can also review some additional opening thoughts that were presented in approach #1 or review the ethical wills contained in Appendix I.

Values and Beliefs

Now that you have an opening, you can move on to the first exercise. The goal of this exercise is to identify the values and beliefs that are important to you. There are a number of phrases that invite completion. Use some or all of them. Don't be surprised if you find yourself writing several paragraphs or more!

To get started, here's a list of commonly held values and beliefs. However, if you think of other values that are more important to you, make your own personal list to work from. If you need more ideas, look at the list presented in the first approach.

- being honest
- keeping your word
- being dependable

- helping others in need
- learning from mistakes
- having a sense of humor

Exercise #1: What's Important to Me?

- What I value most is . . .
- I believe in . . .
- What I did in my life to stand up for my values and beliefs is . . .

Here's an example of something I believe in and what I did to act on my beliefs:

I've always felt that helping others in need and volunteering to support your community are important personal values.

While training to be a physician, I volunteered in a migrant workers clinic. The migrant workers didn't have any health insurance or easy access to medical care. They often went without needed health care in order to support their families. They were so grateful for any medical services, I really felt like I was making a difference in their lives.

I hope you will experience this same feeling of making a difference in other people's lives. There are many opportunities for this. You usually receive more than you give whenever and wherever you volunteer your time to help others in need.

Stories like this say so much more than a simple value statement. They provide a window into your soul, illustrating what gives your life meaning. In addition, such stories provide information about the lives that we've lived. If we never tell our stories, who will? They are too important to risk losing forever. Even if our children remember these stories, our great-grandchildren won't. So it's important to write these down to preserve them.

In addition, recording significant memories, events, mishaps, successes, and your past experiences will help you see the patterns that have shaped your life. For example, write about where you grew up, experiences with your family that stand out in your mind, stories about your jobs, and how you chose your occupation.

For example:

I grew up in Bensonhurst, in Brooklyn, NY. When I was 5 years old, my family moved from an apartment to a two-family house that my uncle bought. As it turned out, my father and his brother married my mother and her sister. It was like having two moms and dads and two more siblings! We were very close as a family. We took family vacations together every summer to the Catskill Mountains in upstate New York.

My grandparents lived a few blocks from our house, so I saw them several times a week. When my grandma was unable to live by herself in her apartment, she moved in with us.

The importance of family was a value that my parents taught to me. I hope you kids will stay close to each other and look after each other after I'm gone.

The intent of Exercises #2 and #3 is to record important events, decisions, and meaningful life experiences.

Here is an example that illustrates personal narrative.

Learning is a lifelong occupation. I love to learn new things all the time. I've found that the more I learn the better understanding I have of others and myself. This has been very important in my work because I encounter a diverse group of people every day.

I worked from the time I was in high school. I sold newspapers, worked in a candy store (that's what they called soda fountains in Brooklyn), and did some office work all through college. I had an opportunity to interact with people from many walks of life. I discovered that I enjoyed interacting with people. I chose an occupation (being a physician) in which I could interact and help a diverse group of people. It's important to choose an occupation that you really enjoy—even if it takes a while to figure out what you want to do.

Exercise #4 is another exercise for which I've provided some starter thoughts. Use these or develop your own, or, if you need more ideas, review the items in approach #1.

Exercise #2: Personal Narratives

IMPORTANT EVENTS

Write about important transitional events in your life as you remember them. After you've written them, see if you can identify values that are illustrated. Another way to undertake this exercise is to choose values, such as love, beauty, truth, justice. Write about experiences in a way that sheds light on your personal perspective.

In the second part of this exercise, I've included a number of writing options. There are phrase completion items, recording of life events and activities, and reflective scenarios to think and write about.

MEANINGFUL OR INSTRUCTIVE LIFE EXPERIENCES

• The lessons I've learned from life are that . . .
• The person who had the biggest impact on who I am as a person and why was . . .

• The event in my life that had the biggest impact on who I am as a person was . . .
• I am most proud of my . . .

Make a record of:
• Activities you devoted time to and why.
• Favorite sayings and examples of how they guided you.

The next three exercises are more reflective in nature and may take more time to complete. You can determine at a later time where you want to fit this material into your ethical will.

Some of the items presented may strike you as sensitive and personal. If it's hard for you to write about these things,

---

Exercise #3: Important Decisions
You Made in Your Life

Think about critical decisions you've made throughout your life. Write in as much detail as you want. Then, ask yourself and record the answers to the following questions:
- Why am I glad I made these decisions?
- In retrospect, what would I have done differently?
- What positive actions can I undertake now to change the situation or circumstances that resulted? (This is a good exercise for healing and repairing relationships.)

---

don't worry. The previous exercises presented in this chapter can help you achieve your goal.

Exercise #4: Hopes for the Future

My hopes or my dreams for you are to:
- continue the family traditions of . . .
- stay involved with . . .
- be successful in . . .
- follow the religious observances of . . .

Exercise #5 is a phrase-completion exercise. This exercise can evoke a strong emotional response. As you think about people who were, or have been, important to you, or who had, or have been, a major impact on your life, strong feelings may emerge. If this occurs, don't be alarmed—it's very natural for this to happen. Complete the phrases with as many thoughts as you wish.

Exercise #5: A Reflective Exercise

- From my grandparents I learned that . . .
- From my parents I learned that . . .
- From my spouse/children/siblings I learned that . . .
- From experience I learned that . . .
- I am grateful for . . .
- My most meaningful religious holiday/experience/tradition is . . .

The next two exercises are "visioning" or "imagining" exercises. They have you thinking about the future. Imagining a future situation can be helpful by putting into focus values that are important to you today. And, it can spur us into taking some action.

Exercise #6: What Will I Miss When I'm Gone?

Write about what you'll miss most after you're gone. Be specific. What are things that only you know about, care about, that will die with you? Slow down, let yourself notice and remember what you don't ordinarily, and realize that when you go, you'll miss it. Begin each sentence with: "I'll miss . . ." Here's an example: "I'll miss the dew on the grass on a summer morning when I pick fresh tomatoes from my front-yard garden."

Here's an example for Exercise #6 to illustrate this point:

During a family discussion we talked about holiday celebrations and special foods that were prepared by the "older generations" in the family. They had these special recipes memorized but not written down. Many of the ingredients were determined by taste rather than by measurement. Realizing that these treasures would be lost and missed when our elder generation died, several nieces and grandchildren signed up for "cooking lessons" with *Baube* (a Yiddish term for Grandma) to record and learn how to make these ethnic specialties, thus ensuring the preservation of one aspect of her legacy.

The last exercise in this series, by confronting your mortality, is useful for identifying your core values and what you hold dear. It creates a personal "call to action" to effect change in how you live your life today. In that sense it is a very meaningful exercise to complete.

> ### *Exercise #7: The Eulogy*
> You are attending a funeral. Familiar people are filing in and sitting down. The eulogy is about to begin. You realize the eulogy is about you. What would you like to hear said about yourself?

Here are some phrases you can use for your conclusion. Refer back to the examples in approach #1, or look at some of the ethical will examples in Appendix I.

Concluding Thoughts

- Thank you for your love and support through the years . . .

- I love you all very much . . .
- Think of me when you . . .

After you've completed several of these exercises, you will have a good working draft for your ethical will. As for organizing what you've written, integrate the material into the general outline. You can also assemble your work in an order that reads well and seems more logical to you.

Approach #3
Starting with a Blank Sheet of Paper

If you select approach #3 as your starting point, you probably have a high-comfort level with writing in a less directed way. This is an open-ended way to compile material for your ethical will.

Collecting Ideas

Keeping a journal or diary is a tried-and-true way to collect ideas. It involves writing things down regualarly over a period of weeks, months, or years. This method is an unstructured and spontaneous way to write about events, thoughts, and feelings that strike you as important, and possibly to discover what you really think or feel about a given situation, relationship, or experience.

Common Techniques for Journaling

- Lists: Pick topics relevant to the task, then write until you've exhausted them. This is an excellent way to mine and unleash both the conscious and unconscious mind.
- Dialoguing: This involves engaging in a dialogue with yourself, a part of yourself, or another person who is, of course, actually not present. This is a good way to examine and explore; to loosen your memory; and perhaps discover or recover information outside your recognized knowledge bank.
- Dreams: If this appeals to you, record your dreams in as much detail as you can. Who knows what's to be gleaned? In addition you can save items like quotes, cartoons, and so forth, that articulate your feelings or illustrate your values.

After you've been writing and collecting "data" for a while, you'll want to take some time to review. Here are some suggestions for organizing the content that you've compiled. As you examine your notes, you'll see salient topics and patterns emerge.

Organizing Your Ideas

- Group similar items together.
- Where you have just a few, but meaningful words, expand the thought into sentences. Logical separate paragraphs should follow.
- Arrange the information in any order that seems comfortable to you under outline headings. (You can use any of the outline categories described in approaches #1 and #2.)
- Add an introduction or opening paragraph and a conclusion, and you have your first draft!
- You may want to set the document aside for several days or even weeks, and then review it.
- Revise your draft as you deem appropriate.

✿　✿　✿

It's been said that a first draft of any document is a necessary evil. Use any of these three approaches to create a draft of your ethical will. Or, invent your own way of doing this by taking suggestions from all of the approaches. My goal is to get you started and for you to be comfortable with the process. And, it's easier and a lot more fun to work on revisions of your ethical will once you've completed your initial draft.

As I described the three approaches, I focused on writing as the means to collect information. However, writing isn't the only way to compile information or to assemble your ethical will. I'll expand on this issue in the next chapter.

Preparing, Caring for, and Sharing Your Ethical Will

If you've read through the information and completed the exercises presented in the previous four chapters, you have likely completed at least a rough draft of your ethical will. You're now in the Completion and Review stages as outlined in Chapter 1.

PREPARING AND PRESERVING YOUR ETHICAL WILL

One of the advantages of living in a technologically advanced society is the plethora of choices when it comes to storing and retrieving information. I've seen ethical wills recorded on audiocassette tapes, videotapes, and CD-ROM disks. These technologies allow for the creation of multimedia presentations that include photographs, voice, film, and writing, all together in one package.

Even though I think all of these ways to preserve your ethical will are fine, I think it's very important to prepare a "hard copy" (either handwritten or printed) of your ethical will as well. Why? Because it's impossible to predict how technology will change in the future. (Do you remember when videocassette recorders [VCRs] first became popular? There were two versions available: "VHS" and "Beta." Unfortunately, "Beta" went the way of the dinosaur, so if you recorded your ethical will on Beta, it would be virtually impossible to retrieve it today.)

The fact that there are ethical will documents preserved from as early as the twelfth century bodes well for the preservation of written ethical wills into the future. It's hard to predict where technology will take us. However, most of us would agree that the written word has demonstrated its staying power. Beyond that, an actual handwritten document carries a value all its own.

So, I encourage you to prepare your ethical will in any way that seems comfortable to you. In addition, create a written copy as well. There's something about reading an ethical will written in the writer's hand that is magical.

The main point is that you should create your ethical will and feel comfortable that with proper care it can be preserved for generations to come. To preserve your written ethical will, you may wish to purchase archival (acid-free) paper. This type of paper is very durable and resists degradation over time. Documents written on archival paper, with proper care, can last for generations. Archival paper isn't very expensive and is readily available in art supply stores. You can store your ethical will in a folder that is also made of archival quality materials.

If you're blessed with artistic ability and want to add an extra personal touch, you might think about drawing or painting a design on blank sheets of archival paper.

SHARING YOUR ETHICAL WILL

Conveying an ethical will was usually a prerogative reserved for the patriarch of the family. Initially, when ethical wills were first transmitted orally, wisdom, blessings, burial instructions, and instructions for living a moral and ethical life would be shared when it was perceived that the death of the author was at hand. Of course, death could (and often would) occur unexpectedly, so this could be a hit-or-miss way of passing on these values. And, as a general rule, the messages were directed almost exclusively to children of the author.

When ethical wills became written documents, they were usually attached to wills of inheritance. Thus, the bequeathing of valuables and values occurred at the same time. As a written document, these ethical wills not only provided advice to the recipients, they also served as a keepsake.

Today ethical wills are being shared more commonly while the author is still alive. Why this shift has occurred is not clear, but it can be discerned from the many reasons for creating one. For a start, the sharing of an ethical will while its author is alive creates opportunities for ongoing dialogue with recipients, and allows for additions and revisions to the ethical will over time.

A number of patients in our home hospice program have chosen to have their ethical will read at their funeral in a ceremonial way. Usually, they had already shared their ethical will with close family members, but wanted a way to share it with others as well.

Ethical wills also provide content for eulogies. I find this interesting in light of the eulogy exercise described in the last chapter as a way to create content for your ethical will. This choice is especially helpful if clergy might not have had a relationship with the deceased or his or her family.

In addition to family and friends, consider the value of sharing with other individuals, such as your physician, attorney, financial planner, and clergy.

A note from the community perspective: I was recently contacted by a woman from Texas who reported a project starting at her church. Congregants there will be asked to create an ethical will and submit a copy to be kept in an archive at the church. Future generations of churchgoers at this congregation will have the opportunity to read about the values, beliefs, and hopes of previous parishioners.

REVIEWING AND RENEWING YOUR ETHICAL WILL

Because the majority of people who create an ethical will share it while they are still alive, there will be opportunities for reviewing and updating the document. When you decide to do this is completely up to you. Most likely, you will want to review and update your ethical will at times of significant change in your life, passing through transitional stages, and even on a scheduled periodic basis. Generally speaking, you'll know when it's time for an update. You can rewrite it if you wish, or you can just add to what you already have written.

To Be Avoided

On occasion, ethical wills have been written that "reach out from the grave" to instill guilt or blame, or to denounce survivors or attempt to control their lives. I think of these ethical wills as being "unethical."

During workshops, I have had discussions with a number of participants about how to deal with this issue. Here's what we've come up with for determining if your ethical will passes the test of being "ethical."

If you find as you read your ethical will that it contains a lot of "you" or "you should" statements, this might be a danger signal. Here's a short excerpt from an ethical will written in the mid-twentieth century that illustrates these points—

> And now, my children, obey the instructions of your father. Know that you have been rebellious for as long as I have known you. You have not been obedient and have not appreciated the benefits I have given you. Your personal conduct and your business practices have caused me vexation and pain.

To be fair to the writer of this ethical will, at a later point in the will he does forgive and pardon his children for their transgressions.

If your ethical will contains "I" statements and stories that convey your values, beliefs, dreams, and life lessons, it's less likely that you are treading on "unethical" ground.

This doesn't mean that you shouldn't be clear in your message, or in pointing out a direction that you *hope* your family and community will follow. Remember that these messages will provide the basis for a cherished legacy rather than one that tries to be coercive.

❁   ❁   ❁

Today, the ethical will tradition is becoming an important part of a continuum of how we choose to create our personal legacy and pass on our values to our family and community. This continuum ranges from the creation of a simple ethical will that might be several paragraphs or pages in length to memoirs containing complete life histories, meaningful stories, and life reflections.

Because of their simplicity, ethical wills can be either the primary vehicle for the creation of a personal legacy or just the first step in creating something more involved. One thing is certain: When you have completed your ethical will, you will have gone through a process that can be truly life changing.

6

Living Wills

In March 2005 on a sunny Sunday afternoon, Sandy (my wife), Sophie (my mother-in-law), and I were eager participants in the St. Croix Valley's food-shelf fundraiser "The Chocolate March." As we drove along Wisconsin country roads, visiting several sponsoring bed-and-breakfasts that offered tours of their facilities—and, of course, many varieties of chocolate!—Sophie broke a short silence with these words: "Barry, promise me that you won't let happen to me what's happening to Terri Schiavo. I want you to promise me that you won't let that happen to me."

On that particular Sunday the world, or at least the United States, was witness to the tortuous conclusion of the longest contested legal health-related case in the history of the United States—that of Terri Schiavo.

In 1990, Terri, a young woman in her midtwenties, suffered a cardiac arrest that resulted in severe irreversible brain damage. She required artificial feeding and hydration to survive.

Terri's husband and parents publicly and bitterly disagreed about what treatments Terri would want, given her condition. Daily newspaper, television, and radio reports documented the struggle between them—a struggle that would involve not only the Florida judicial, legislative, and executive branches of government but also the Supreme Court, Congress, and even the president of the United States.

Terri's fifteen-year odyssey of surviving in a persistent vegetative state ended when her husband was allowed to make the decision to discontinue the feeding tube that had kept her alive for many years. Her peaceful death occurred two weeks after the withdrawal of her artificial nutrition and hydration.

Why did this situation occur?

The main reason this happened was that Terri did not have a living will—a document that identifies an individual's wishes, goals, and treatment preferences in specific medical situations.

A living will is also known as a *health care directive* or an *advance care plan*. When properly prepared, living wills provide useful information to family and health care providers to guide treatment choices and preferences. Living wills can also identify a *health care proxy*—someone designated to speak on behalf of a person who is unable to speak for herself or himself. This is also known as a *health care agent* or *durable power of attorney for health care decisions*.

Without Terri's living will, the door was left open for different opinions about what Terri would have wanted, given her specific medical situation. And that is exactly what happened. Terri's husband had one opinion and Terri's parents had an opposing opinion. With no health care proxy named, it was inevitable that the courts would decide who the proxy decision maker would be.

Can this type of situation be avoided and, if so, how?

The answer is yes—most of the time. The decision that was made by Terri's husband, Michael, is made hundreds of times every day. These decisions are not "newsworthy" when an individual makes her or his wishes known in advance, to which family members agree or at least agree to respect, even if they have differing opinions and feelings.

In the following pages, I walk you through these different aspects of living wills:

- What is a living will?
- Why write a living will? (and what can happen if you don't)
- What to include in a living will
- Common misunderstandings about living wills
- When to write a living will
- How to write your living will and make it a legal document
- With whom to share your living will
- Reviewing and updating your living will

Examples of actual living wills (including my own) are in Appendix IV so that you have a realistic sense of what they are like. You'll see that they needn't be complicated or hard to complete. You can use one of several living will worksheets; some samples are included in Appendix V. Finally, I review the complementary nature of living wills and ethical wills.

WHAT IS A LIVING WILL?

As mentioned, living wills are also called *health care directives* and *advance care plans*. A living will is a document that spells out, in advance, the medical treatments you want when your medical condition requires treatment decisions and you are unable to communicate your wishes to your health care provider. In addition to describing your medical treatment preferences, a living will identifies a health care proxy— someone that you choose to speak for you and to make decisions for you if you are unable to speak for yourself. Living wills do not take the place of your right to make decisions affecting the delivery of health care to you as long as you are able to make and communicate those decisions.

Options for medical treatments can be as simple as wanting to be kept comfortable or having an antibiotic medication for an infection. You also have options for more complicated treatments, such as those involving mechanical respirators (commonly known as *ventilators* or *artificial breathing machines*), which breathe for you, or artificial nutrition and hydration using a feeding tube.

Living wills are considered to be legal documents, just like a will of inheritance (or last will and testament). Many state bar associations have forms to assist you in the preparation of a living will; however, you don't have to hire a lawyer to draw up a living will. In most states, having two witnesses sign the document or having the document notarized will make it legal.

Because laws differ from one state to another, you need to know how to make your living will a legal document in the state where you live.

WHY WRITE A LIVING WILL?
(AND WHAT CAN HAPPEN IF YOU DON'T)

My patients say that the three most important reasons for writing a living will are

- "Maintaining personal control over what happens to me in serious medical situations"
- "Relieving the burden on my family from having to make difficult medical decisions"
- "Assisting health care providers in offering treatment options that are best for me in a particular situation"

People have many other personal reasons for wanting to write a living will. Some have gone through difficult and unpleasant situations with loved ones who didn't have living wills and who never discussed what they would want done in specific circumstances. Others are encouraged or convinced by their family, doctor, lawyer, financial advisor, or clergy that having a living will on the record is important. All of these are good reasons for completing a living will document; however, the best reason for doing so is to avoid what can happen if you don't have one and you are unable to make your own decisions.

If you don't have a living will and a health care proxy named, state laws determine who will be the proxy. Although many states have similar rules for appointing a proxy (for example, first a spouse, then adult children, then parents), there are differences, and because this is a legal proceeding, the results can be unpredictable. Here is an example of what happened to one of my patients several years ago.

Jim was a hospice patient with advanced cancer who lapsed into a coma and couldn't eat or drink. Jim never completed a living will, and he didn't name a health care proxy either. It was unlikely that Jim would ever recover or regain consciousness. Given the medical situation, Jim's wife (from a second marriage) just wanted Jim to be kept comfortable and to "let nature take its course." Jim's parents thought otherwise. They hoped a miracle would happen if they kept Jim going. They wanted a feeding tube placed to keep their son alive as long as possible.

In most cases, under Minnesota state laws, the spouse is appointed as the proxy. However, the parents (who never liked the second wife) made the case to the judge that Jim's spouse wanted him to die because she wanted to collect the insurance money as soon as possible. Persuaded by this argument, the judge appointed Jim's mother as the health care proxy. As a result, a feeding tube was so ordered and put in place. Because Jim's cancer was so advanced, he only lived for a few days in spite of the feeding tube. Nevertheless, a difficult situation resulted, including hard feelings between Jim's wife and parents at a time of loss for all of them.

Fortunately, this type of situation doesn't always happen in the absence of a living will. Most often, families rally around their loved one and are able to agree on the best course of action. However, if there's no living will you can never be sure. For example, an estranged child may appear and insist (perhaps out of guilt) that "everything possible must be done to keep my mother/father alive." This can lead down a path similar to the one taken by Jim and his family.

It's better to be safe than sorry, and, as you'll see, completing a living will isn't unusually difficult.

WHAT TO INCLUDE IN YOUR LIVING WILL

Most living will forms and worksheets contain two or three sections:

- One section describes your medical treatment preferences.
- Another section identifies the person whom you choose to be your health care agent or proxy.

- A third section explains where you can express additional thoughts and requests, such as staying at home with family and friends, sharing values, and so on.

In my opinion, the most important thing you can do is to name someone to speak for you if or when you can't speak for yourself. This individual is called a *health care proxy, health care agent,* or *durable power of attorney for health care decisions.* Why is naming a proxy so important? Because living wills can get lost, misinterpreted, or even ignored. Your proxy will be your advocate when this support is most needed.

When you name a health care proxy, choose someone whom you believe will follow through with your wishes in the event that you are unable to make decisions or speak for yourself. This can happen if you are unconscious, in a coma, or have advanced dementia, such as that resulting from Alzheimer's disease. Most people choose a family member or a friend. In my case, I chose my wife as my proxy. I also named my adult daughters as proxies if my wife is unable to fulfill that role. You can grant your proxy the power to make decisions that are different from the ones that you spell out in advance. In some states, if you do not grant this flexibility in decision making to your proxy, then your written directives must be strictly followed.

After you name a health care proxy, focus on common medical treatment choices in serious health situations. Although it's impossible to list all of the possibilities in any particular situation, here's a short list of common treatments that you may have to make decisions about in serious illness situations.

I've included a short explanation or description of these treatments along with additional information about the pros and cons (or benefits and burdens) of these treatments. Thanks to popular medical television shows, we see overly optimistic outcomes of many treatments in serious medical situations. We need to realize that television is fiction and often portrays unrealistic medical results, very different from what happens in real life. We need to understand that all medical treatments have burdens and risks as well as benefits.

1. Cardiopulmonary resuscitation (CPR)

CPR is used when your heart stops beating (cardiac arrest) or you stop breathing (respiratory arrest). A number of things might be tried to get your heart beating and yourself breathing. They include

- Electrical cardioversion (or defibrillation): an external electrical shock applied to the chest wall in an effort to establish a normal heart rhythm.

- External cardiac massage: compressing the heart externally by forcibly pressing down on the breastbone in an effort to pump blood through the body.
- Intubation: inserting a plastic tube into the trachea (windpipe) and attaching one end of the tube to an external oxygen source in an effort to deliver oxygen into the lungs. When this treatment is combined with external cardiac massage, the blood receives oxygen as it is pumped through the body.

When addressing CPR, you make a decision about whether you do or do not want to be resuscitated or intubated. If you don't want to be resuscitated or intubated, specify "Do not resuscitate" (DNR) or "Do not intubate" (DNI).

- Pros and cons:

    The obvious benefit of CPR is that if it's successful, you're still alive. But you should be aware of the success rate of CPR. In a hospital setting, the chances of surviving CPR and being discharged home are about 15 percent. Those who survive typically have just had a heart attack and are otherwise in pretty good health. For the elderly and those with chronic illnesses, the success rate is even less. What about CPR performed by an emergency medical technician (EMT) or ambulance crew? Out-of-hospital CPR survival is about 5 percent. CPR attempted in a nursing home setting has a success rate of almost zero percent.

2. Artificial feeding and hydration

Artificial feeding and hydration is a medical treatment used when you can no longer take in enough food and water to meet your body's nutritional needs or when you can't swallow properly and start choking whenever you try to eat or drink. This situation can occur as an expected consequence of an advancing illness such as some cancers, or it could be a permanent or temporary condition following a stroke.

In these situations, a decision needs to be made about whether to insert a feeding tube, which is done surgically by inserting a tube through the wall of the abdomen, into the stomach. Once the tube is in place, a small balloon on the tip of the tube is inflated to prevent the tube from slipping out. Nutritional formulas flow through the feeding tube into the stomach. Water or other fluids can be given through the feeding tube as well.

- Pros and cons:
  The main benefit of artificial feeding and fluids is that it provides the sustenance we need to keep us alive. This can be critically important in medical situations that may

be temporary—for example, in the first few days or weeks after a stroke. Artificial feeding and fluids can be a burden in nonreversible situations, such as that during advancing cancer that's no longer responding to treatment and the end stages of advanced dementia.

Because cancer cells are the fastest growing cells in the body, they have the highest nutritional requirements. They will utilize the lion's share of calories that are introduced into the body. As a result, artificial feeding in most cases of advanced cancer rarely contributes to longevity.

In dementia, tube feeding is often offered as a choice when food can't be properly chewed or swallowed. When this happens, the food can go down the windpipe, into the lungs, and cause a type of pneumonia known as *aspiration pneumonia*. In cases of advanced dementia, feeding tubes do not decrease the incidence of aspiration pneumonia, nor do they improve survival.

The most significant concern that I've heard from patients and their families facing the decision regarding artificial feeding and fluids is that they believe that their loved ones will painfully starve to death or die of thirst. This is not the case. In medical situations such as those described here, the body responds by producing substances called *endorphins,* which keep you comfortable while other body functions and systems slow down and stop altogether. As we saw in the Terri Schiavo situation, she lapsed into a coma and died peacefully within a couple of weeks of her artificial feeding and fluids being stopped.

3. Intravenous (IV) treatment

IV is a medical treatment used to deliver medications and special fluids directly into your vein in order to maintain hydration. In preparation for IV treatments, a special kind of needle is inserted into a vein and taped to the skin so that it stays in place. The decision to be made is whether you want an IV.

* Pros and cons:

    If medicines can't be taken by mouth, IVs are a useful way to administer medication for treatment (such as an antibiotic for infections) and comfort (medication for pain or nausea). IVs can also provide fluids for hydration. The main burdens of IV treatments are the discomfort caused by insertion of the needle into the vein and the possibility of infection at the IV site or in the bloodstream. In addition, too much fluid can be put into your circulatory system, causing swelling and discomfort in different parts of the body and gurgly breathing sounds caused by fluid buildup in the lungs (pulmonary edema) with accompanying difficulty breathing.

4. Blood transfusions

Certain medical conditions cause a low red blood cell count (called *anemia*). When anemia is severe, you may experience weakness and shortness of breath. Sometimes, blood transfusions are used to temporarily relieve these symptoms. Other reasons for blood transfusions include the loss of blood secondary to a traumatic injury. The decision to be made is whether you want a transfusion.

- Pros and cons:
   The main benefit is that blood transfusions can relieve the symptoms described here. One burden is that you can have a severe allergic reaction to blood transfusions. In the past, there was a danger of contracting HIV or AIDS from blood transfusions. Because of new blood-screening techniques, this problem has been virtually eliminated as a risk. In general, you need to go to a hospital or outpatient clinic to have a transfusion. This can be a significant inconvenience.

5. Antibiotics

Antibiotics are medications that are used to fight infections caused by different bacteria. In acute illnesses (such as bladder infections, ear infections, bronchitis) antibiotics are commonly used. The decision to be made is whether you want to use antibiotics.

- Pros and cons:

    In situations of advanced illness, antibiotics can be beneficial in the relief of symptoms caused by relatively minor infections (like those just mentioned). However, it's not uncommon to develop serious infections as part of the natural course of a progressive advanced illness, and an antibiotic may not be effective in these cases. If you are unable to take an antibiotic by mouth, it must be administered through an IV, with the associated discomfort and risks that I have already described. Also, the use of an antibiotic can result in secondary infections that are resistant to antibiotic treatment.

6. Surgery and other diagnostic tests

In some medical situations, surgical treatments can be a reasonable option. Because these are so individualized, I won't go into detail. Surgeons will review the benefits and burdens of any proposed surgery as part of the informed consent process. If there's something in the explanation about the surgery that you don't understand, be sure to ask questions so that you are given information about the surgery in language that you can understand. Only then can you make an informed choice.

Similarly, if further tests are recommended, make sure you understand why they are being ordered and how their results affect treatment choices.

- Pros and cons:
    The benefits and burdens of surgery and other diagnostic tests relate to your overall goals. If the proposed surgery or tests support your goals, that's a good reason to proceed with the recommendation. If they don't support your overall goals, they may become a burden.

7. Comfort-focused care

Almost everyone wants to be cured, if that's possible; however, many chronic illnesses can't be cured. If these illnesses limit our activities or ability to function independently or if symptoms of these illnesses are distressing and disabling, you may want to redirect the treatment from one that focuses on efforts to cure or control your illness to one that focuses efforts on relieving symptoms, easing suffering, and improving your quality of life.

Comfort-focused care can be used for all medical conditions. This care usually addresses common symptoms such as pain, breathing difficulty, nausea and vomiting, and so on. Comfort-focused treatments can be used by themselves, or they can be used with all other treatments. There's no reason why you have to be uncomfortable or distressed with certain symptoms if you don't want to be.

- Pros and cons:
  Relief of pain, shortness of breath, nausea, vomiting, and other distressing physical symptoms are the main benefits of comfort-focused care. When medical treatments shift to a comfort focus, hospice can be an ideal option for you and your family. Burdens may arise in the form of side effects to some of the medications used to relieve troubling symptoms. Common side effects include drowsiness, nausea, and constipation. If IVs were needed to administer medications, the previously described risks would apply.

8. Miscellaneous items

You can include other items in your living will. In addition to naming specific medical treatments, you can also state your preferences, such as wanting to stay at home and not go to the hospital or having family and friends with you as much of the time as possible when you are very ill. Some living will documents provide a place to talk about your values (such as in an ethical will) and to thank people for the role they played in your life and in your care.

Common Misunderstandings about Living Wills

Over the years, I have learned from my patients a number of common misunderstandings about living wills. I'd like to share some of these with you so that you have the real story about living wills.

One common misunderstanding is that many people don't realize that a treatment can be used on a trial basis for several days or weeks. If the treatment isn't working, it can be stopped. For example, in a situation where you have an acute stroke and you can't eat, drink, communicate with anybody, or respond to anybody, it's OK to try artificial nutrition and hydration (and a feeding tube) for several days or a week to see if there's any improvement. If there is, you can continue the treatment; if things get worse or if there's no change in your condition and your doctor believes that there is little chance of further recovery, you may want to have the feeding tube stopped and let nature take its course. You can see how I address these situations in my personal living will (see p. 175).

A second common misunderstanding is that many people don't realize that they can change their mind about what treatments they want as their condition changes. As long as you have the ability to make your own decisions (called *decision-making capacity*), you can change your mind. What do I mean by decision-making capacity? This means that you understand your medical condition, you understand your choices for medical treatment, and you understand what might happen based on your choices. This is also called *informed consent* in medical terminology.

A third misunderstanding about living wills involves health care providers. In emergency situations when your primary care doctor may not be available, health care providers may assume that if you've taken the time to write a living will, it means that you probably don't want treatments such as CPR. That's why it's important for you, your family members, and your close friends to have copies of your living will. If you have a copy of your living will available when you seek medical attention, doctors and nurses can better understand what your preferences are.

You also need to know that if you have a living will and call 911 for an emergency situation, your wishes may be ignored. Why is that? Because the law in many states requires emergency medical personnel to do everything they can to sustain life (for example, doing CPR), even if you have a living will that specifically states that you don't want CPR.

Fortunately, you can do something to prevent this from happening. You can ask your physician to write specific orders regarding certain treatment on a prescription pad for you. This is called *physician orders for scope of treatment,* or POST. Here's how it works. If my patient Mrs. Jones doesn't want CPR, I would write on a prescription pad "Do not perform CPR on Mrs. Jones" and sign my name. If this is shown to the EMTs who arrive on the scene when 911 is called, they will honor her preferences. This is another good reason why your primary care doctor should not only know that you have a living will but also have a copy of it.

Finally, there's a huge misunderstanding about who should bring up the subject of writing a living will. Several years ago at a medical conference, I heard a speaker present research that showed that physicians believe that their patients will bring up the idea of writing a living will. Patients, on the other hand, said that it's the physician's role to start the discussion about living wills. This is probably why so few people have written a living will (estimated at 15 percent to 20 percent of the adult population). This has created a situation where the patient and the doctor are each waiting for the other person to bring up the subject of living wills, time runs out, the office visit is over, and nothing happens. Coincidently, this situation is changing.

More and more physicians and physicians in training are being educated about the importance of discussing living wills with their patients. In addition, many lawyers who prepare estate plans routinely offer to draft a living will for their clients. I know mine did, though I was a step ahead of him!

Because of the publicity of the Terri Schiavo case, many people are realizing the importance of bringing up this subject and having meaningful conversations with their families, health care providers, and estate planning professionals.

When to Write a Living Will

The best answers are "right now" or "anytime's a good time." However, the urgency is higher during certain times than other times. The highest priority is if you have any serious or advanced medical illness. Examples include illnesses such as heart failure, cancer, and chronic lung disease. Next on my priority list is if you're seventy-five years old or older—even if you are in top shape. As we get older, our memory may not be as sharp as it used to be. As we continue to age, we may find ourselves in situations in which we can't make informed decisions. And once that happens, it's too late.

Another good time to bring up this subject is the next time you see your doctor for a checkup. There's a good chance that your doctor may beat you to the punch on bringing up the subject. But don't leave this to chance. It's just too important.

How to Write Your Living Will and Make It a Legal Document

You may be surprised to learn that writing a living will is easier than you think. The reason is that a number of resources are readily available and include easy-to-use worksheets and living will forms. These are helpful because they ensure that all of the important items are included in your living will.

Many of them are available at no cost. Some organizations charge a small fee to use their materials. A couple of helpful Web sites include www.partnershipforcaring.org and www .agingwithdignity.org. Some sample forms are included in Appendix V. If you prefer, you can write a living will that suits your personal style, as long as you make sure that you follow through and make it a legal document. That's what I did with my living will.

Here are five simple steps you can follow to ensure that you complete your living will.

1. Make sure you understand all of your medical conditions and illnesses. It is hard to identify the kinds of treatments you want if you do not understand your medical conditions to begin with. If you have questions about your medical illness, it's a good idea to ask your doctor to explain things in a language that you understand.
2. Identify what's most important to you as it relates to your medical conditions. Review the four examples of living wills in Appendix IV so that you know what they look like when completed. Look at the questions on some of the living will forms in Appendix V. This will help you to identify your wishes and preferences and how you want to state them in your living will document.
3. Have conversations with family members about your preferences, and don't forget to include your health care proxy if you know who you want to ask that person

to be (see step 4). You can clear up misunderstandings, and your family will know exactly what your wishes are. I know that in some cases this may be difficult or impossible to accomplish. Do the best you can.

4. Name your health care proxy, someone whom you want to speak for you if you can't speak for yourself. It's extremely important to have a conversation with any potential proxy candidate to make sure that she or he is willing and able to carry out your wishes if called upon.

   Choosing a proxy can be a difficult and sensitive issue with family members. I've seen situations when the proxy (usually an adult child) was unable to follow the wishes of the parent. This usually involved a circumstance where the parent (the patient) did not want life-prolonging treatments if they were unlikely to improve the overall situation. The proxy couldn't accept the parent's wishes because she or he didn't want to lose the parent. In some cases you may need to name a proxy who isn't a close relative. If your preferred proxy isn't sure about taking on the responsibility, you both can review your living will to make sure she or he is comfortable following through with your preferences if a situation should ever arise.

5. Complete one of the living will worksheets or make up your own document. If you need guidance, call your physician's office for advice. Check with your attorney's office or call your state bar association to find out what

you need to do to make your living will document legal. For example, many states require two witnesses to sign your document, or you can have it notarized.

WITH WHOM TO SHARE YOUR LIVING WILL

Once completed, be sure that copies of your living will are in the hands of people who are most likely to be participating in a situation in which the will is needed. You should keep a copy of your living will with you at all times, if possible (even in the glove compartment of your car!). Give copies to your health care proxy, spouse, children, parents, primary care doctor, nurse practitioner, specialists, attorney, estate planner, and clergy. I recommend that you review your living will with your primary care physician. A good time to do so would be at a scheduled visit for a checkup. Otherwise, you can set up a specific appointment to review your living will. I also suggest that you have your health care proxy come with you for this doctor's appointment so that you, your proxy, and your doctor cover the same information at the same time and have any questions answered.

Why share your living will with so many people? The main reason living will preferences are ignored is that your living will isn't available at the time a decision needs to be made.

And if you are unable to communicate your wishes and your proxy can't be located, the default decision usually involves doing everything to keep a person alive. This happens a lot.

To deal with the problem of access, some businesses provide access to your living will twenty-four hours a day, seven days per week. When using them, you usually have an identification card or bracelet that alerts health care providers that your living will is accessible. In the future, it's likely that computerized "smart cards" (which look like credit cards) will have information pertaining to your insurance, medical history, medications, allergies, and living will readily available. Your living will can be accessed by scanning the card. That is futuristic thinking. Until it happens, I strongly encourage you to provide a copy of your witnessed or notarized document to all the people listed here.

REVIEWING AND UPDATING YOUR LIVING WILL

I have mentioned that you could change your mind about your medical treatment preferences anytime. Reviewing your living will choices is a good idea during at least the following four times.

1. Whenever your medical condition worsens.

2. If your living situation changes—for example, if you can no longer live independently and need to move to an assisted living facility or a nursing home.
3. On a periodic basis—for example, during a periodic physical checkup with your health care provider or on your birthday (everyone remembers her or his birthday, but some people put off going to the doctor).
4. Per state law—some states require updating your living will on a periodic basis. If your living will is out of date, it may be invalid. Check your state laws!

At these times, you need to take out your copy of your living will and walk through the different situations in the document. If everything fits for you, that's all you need to do. If something seems out of date or doesn't apply to you anymore, then it's important to make any changes so that your living will reflects your current wishes and preferences. Of course, if you make changes, you need to have your document witnessed/notarized and dated. Then, you need to send updated copies to the people to whom you sent your original or previous living will—especially your proxy!

You'll find a certain peace of mind once you've completed your living will. Your living will makes the statement that you've thought about the things that could happen to you and that you're expressing your wishes and preferences in advance . . . just in case. In addition, you will have given your family a wonderful gift, relieving them of the burden of potentially difficult decisions by providing the necessary guidance to make those decisions if you are unable to.

THE RELATIONSHIP BETWEEN LIVING WILLS AND ETHICAL WILLS

Although ethical wills are more than three thousand years older than living wills, the two have a strong connection. From a historical perspective, ethical wills often specified burial instructions for the family to follow. Today, it's not uncommon to have statements about burial and funeral preferences contained in a living will.

The strongest link between ethical wills and living wills relates to the fact that both documents are based on our values and beliefs. Themes commonly addressed in an ethical will include what we find meaningful and significant and what we hope for, whereas the focus of a living will is on our wishes, preferences, and goals.

A living will is written to inform the future about what we believe today. An ethical will provides a bridge from the past to the future. While your living will sends the message "I care about you and don't want to burden you with these difficult decisions," ethical wills, as "the voice of the heart," will provide lasting comfort to your loved ones. Having both of these documents will be a blessing for those you care about.

Knowing what you value will help to clarify what treatment options would be best in your specific situation. I've seen families struggle with the many options available for prolonging the quantity of life that don't address the issue of quality of life. And I've seen the relief within families who can more easily let go when Grandma has written in her ethical will that "I've led a good and full life, I believe in the hereafter, I'm not afraid to move on, and I want you all to know that I love you very much."

Appendix I
Voices of the Heart:
Modern Ethical Wills

This appendix contains examples of authentic modern ethical wills. They represent a diversity of styles, format, length, contents, age of the author, or a compelling story behind the creation of the ethical will. Most were written within the last ten years.

The examples are arranged, by decade, based on the age of the authors. Each ethical will is preceded by a brief introduction. The authors themselves, family members, or close friends wrote some of the introductions.

Ideally, the range of examples will help to build your confidence in your ability to write your own ethical will. I hope you will be able to relate closely with one or more examples. As you will see by the diversity of these examples, there is no one way to write an ethical will.

Ethical Wills
by Authors in Their Twenties

Bettina Brickell was twenty-nine years old when she died. This
letter to her family and friends was read at her memorial service.

Dear Friends and Loved Ones,

*As I contemplated this memorial service, I felt great grati-
tude in my heart that each of you would be here to say good-
bye to me. Many of you have shared your warmth, kindness
and love with me during these last months. I want to say
thank you and good-bye and share with you the lessons I've
learned through my dying.*

*I have profoundly experienced that love is all that matters.
Like many people, I occasionally got caught in my pettiness
and separation, thinking I knew the right answer. I judged others and I have judged myself even more harshly. But I have
learned that we carry within ourselves the abundant wisdom
and love to heal our weary heart and judgmental mind.*

*During the time of my illness, I have loved more deeply. My
heart feels as if it has exploded. I do not carry anger. I feel we
are all doing the best we can. Judging others closes the heart
and when one is dying, that is a waste of precious sharing. Life
is how we stand in relationship to both ourselves and to others.
Loving and helping each other are all that is important.*

*We are in the fall season. I feel privileged to die as the
leaves fall from the trees. There is a naturalness to the cycle of*

life and death and for whatever reason, it is my time to die, even though I am young. It is OK. It is right and natural. Life is not about how long we live, but about how we live, and I have had a good life. I accept my dying as part of the wondrous process of life.

My sadness is in leaving you. I'll miss the deep comfort and love of gently waking up in (my husband) Peter's arms, giving up our dreams of future years together. I'll miss the sunny days of fishing with my dad, of sharing with my mom her love of life and cosmopolitan savoir-faire. I'll miss giggling with my sister, Maria, over life's impasses. How appreciative I feel when I think of my brother Michael's faith and encouragement of me.

As I lay dying, I think of all of you, each special in your own way, that I have loved and shared this life with. I reluctantly give up walking on this beautiful planet, where every step is a prayer. The glistening sun on the trees, the sound of a brook as it makes its way down the mountain, the serenity and beauty of a gentle snowfall, sitting at the rim of a Utah canyon and catching a glimpse of eternity—these are the things I have loved.

Please do not think I have lost a battle with cancer, for I have won the challenge of life. I have shared unconditional love. I have opened to the mystery of Spirit and feel that divinity is all around us every day and provides us with a path on which our spirit may take flight.

Chief Crazy Horse said upon his final battle, "It is a good day to die because all the things of my life are present." That

*is how I feel as I think of the abundance, adventure, opportu-
nity and love in my life.*

*When you think of me, know that my spirit has taken flight
and that I loved you.*

With my love, Bettina

ETHICAL WILLS BY
AUTHORS IN THEIR THIRTIES

I wrote this to my then fourteen-year-old son while he was
away at Confirmation camp. I was thirty-eight at the time and
had been remarried for almost three years. Until that point I
was a single mom who got divorced when he was three. (I also
have another son. At the time I got divorced he was one.) My
fourteen-year-old chose to go live with his dad and step mom so
he could attend a different high school. It was an amicable decision all around as they only live five miles from me.

I didn't really start this to be an "ethical will" but when I look
at it, it is just that! Kind of cool! I love the concept. I'm now in
the process of writing my youngest, who is now fourteen, and
starting high school . . . and moving to his dad's as well. I'm going to be an empty nester at forty-one. Yow!

Dear Jason

I love you! Yep, I do! But, you should know this by now!

I can't believe you are starting high school in a week or so.

*I remember high school so vividly—as a time of anxiety, fun,
experimenting and most of all friendships. It was all too clear*

to me how important high school was to me at my 20-year reunion a couple of weeks ago. And, I am a bit sad that you won't be living with me throughout these years, but I am also glad that you have such a great relationship with dad and Cindy. Just remember that I am ALWAYS here for you—no matter where you are. It might seem strange to you to come to me with your problems, or concerns, or joys . . . but you can, anytime. You really can tell me anything. I may "wig out" at first, you know me, after I calm down I can be downright rational and have good advice!

Throughout your 14 years I have tried to be the best mom I can be. I haven't always succeeded, but I think I've done pretty darn well! As a single mom for so much of your life, it hasn't always been easy. Luckily I have a wonderful support system that got me through the tough times. I apologize for the times that I wasn't the mom you would have liked.

Teenagers can be real pains in the butt (I'm sure I was) but they soon grow out of it and become pretty neat adults! I hope through your teenage years I can look past the irritating times and see your goodness. And I hope you can appreciate the things I need to do, as a mom, to help you grow into the best possible adult you can be. There will be times you will "hate" me because of my rules or advice . . . but I can handle that because I know you will see why I have to do some of the things I do once you are older. Hang in there with Mark, dad, Cindy, and me during those times when you think we are "out of it."

Jason, you are one neat kid! Really! I appreciate your sense of humor and your kindness. I am so darn proud to call you my kid . . . and so darn proud to be your mom!

Confirmation is a big step. It is one step closer in your walk with Christ. In those times when you think no one is on your side, He is. Pray and praise God. You will rely on Him throughout your entire life. I know I do.

I love you, Jason.

Mom

By Elaine Ellis-Stone

When I was pregnant with our first child I often found myself daydreaming about the future and the myriad challenges of motherhood. Before we were even married, my husband, Paul, and I had discussed the values we wanted to instill in our child. But our discussions didn't seem concrete to me. I feared that the important ideas we agreed upon could easily be lost once we became engulfed in the daily tasks of parenting. I wanted some way to capture our thoughts to make them more lasting and real.

At the same time Paul and I were formulating our theories on parenting, I was participating in the Hadassah Leadership Academy, a forum for study of Jewish women's history and leadership. As part of our studies, we read the ethical will of Gluckel of Hameln. This document is one of the few that sheds light on Jewish women's lives in medieval times. Gluckel, a mother of many children in 17th century Germany, recorded the major events in her often tragic life, what she learned from them and the values she held dear and wanted to pass on to her children. Writing an ethical will is common in Jewish tradition, I learned, and offers a window onto a specific time in history as well as how certain Jewish values transcend time.

Being a writer, I tend to feel my ideas become concrete by writing them down. Not only does writing help me clarify my thoughts; it also gives me something tangible to return to over time to measure how my thinking has evolved. The discussions Paul and I were having about parenting and the study I was doing with Hadassah converged and prompted me to write an ethical will to my unborn child.

In it I set down a little about my family's history and what I feel is important to pass on to the next generation. Because Paul is not Jewish, I felt a special need to convey the richness of Judaism and how both Paul and I want our child to be raised as a Jew. After completing the ethical will I felt all our talk about values and parenting had been crystallized into a valuable document that will serve as our guide once we are in the thick of caring for a child.

From the examples we studied in my Hadassah group, ethical wills traditionally are written in retrospect. A parent may reflect back over their life, picking out the most important lessons learned to pass on to his or her family. I see my will more as a work in progress. I hope to update it as our child grows and reaches other milestones in life.

Four months after completing my will, we had a baby girl—Rachael. Already we've fulfilled one promise I made—to give her a Hebrew name. Ultimately, of course, the ethical will is just words on paper. The real proof of our parenting and our values is in Rachael.

Here is the ethical will written by Elaine, 38 years old, to her as yet unborn child during her pregnancy.

To my unborn child:

I am writing this in eager anticipation of your birth. I know that I have much to learn about being a parent. I'm sure the challenges will be greater than even now I can imagine, and the rewards are probably bigger than I can fathom at this point.

Please know that you are a cherished being whom your father and I have waited half a lifetime to meet. We're so excited about your birth and everything that will come afterward.

I write this to you now, knowing that my perspective may change as you grow and develop as an individual and as I grow as a parent. Your father and I are becoming parents later in life, with many experiences and, I hope, a little wisdom gained from them. I know we still have much to learn. But this is what I know so far and what I hope for you in the future.

First, know that you will have a unique perspective because you are Jewish, but you also will have your father's culture and traditions. Consider yourself doubly blessed with this wide vista from which to view the world. Even though your father is not Jewish, we agree that it is important for you to be raised as a Jew. You will naturally absorb the secular culture around you. Learning what it means to be Jewish in this world will be more difficult and may be a continually on-going quest, just as it is for me.

As parents, we want you to be knowledgeable about Judaism and to appreciate your religion and history. You will see that there are many wonderful customs and beliefs. Thousands of years of wisdom are contained in the rituals and ceremonies of Judaism that can guide you throughout your life.

Remember, you are forever linked to this long and rich history. As a reminder of this, we are choosing a Hebrew name for you.

The world your father and I live in is mainly a secular, liberal world. While your dad doesn't identify with any religion, I always knew I was Jewish even though my mother and father are not particularly observant. I do remember my Grandpa Sol, your great-grandfather, telling stories about being chased by Cossacks, and hiding in haystacks during the pogroms. Even after his family settled in Eveleth, Minnesota, the Finnish miners' kids bullied grandpa and his brothers.

Your great-grandma Gantz' parents fled Kiev, Russia to settle in the wilds of Saskatchewan and trade with the Indians. Often the stories I heard about being Jewish were about the hardships that Jews endured just because they were different.

Our family has become very assimilated and lost touch with many of the religious traditions, but we identify ourselves as Jews and are proud of that fact. Judaism is your foundation, but it is also important to be part of the larger world. While our Jewish ancestors may have lived in fear, confined to the Jewish community or later sought to bury their identity when they ventured out into the world, I hope you will be proud of who you are and find a trusted community beyond Judaism.

Cultivate a diversity of friends and remember to judge a person as an individual, not by their ethnic, religious or racial group. Be sincere and honest and learn to recognize these qualities in others. Call these people your friends. Be aware of the evils of the world, but do not be consumed by them. Don't let them stunt what I hope will be your adventuresome spirit and desire to taste all the wonderful things the world has to offer.

By adventuresome spirit I don't necessarily mean white water rafting or backpacking through Mongolia, although if that is what your heart desires, then I would say to do it. By being adventuresome, I really mean be broad-minded and curious about the world. I hope that you will have a passion for learning. In school, learn for the sake of learning and not with an eye only to a future career or how much money you can make. Hard work and a broad understanding will bring success. Ultimately consider yourself successful if you sit back at the end of the day and reflect with a sense of pride and satisfaction on your behavior and accomplishments— both personal and professional—for that day.

Remember you will learn more by listening than by speaking. Be observant, but don't just be an observer. Be confident and proud of what you can offer to the world. This means knowing your strengths as well as your flaws. The only way you can truly know yourself is to embrace life fully and in a balanced way. Enrich your mind, exercise your body, and feed your spirit with music, art, meaningful work, friends and helping the community at large.

I hope that you, just as I do, will continually strive to achieve these ideals. I apologize in advance for any shortcomings I may have as a parent. I promise I will try to be-

come aware of them and to correct them. And I look forward
to learning from and about you.

Love, Mom 3/7/99

ETHICAL WILLS BY
AUTHORS IN THEIR FORTIES

Lisa wrote this to her son for his "golden birthday."

March 13, 2002
Dear Ted,
Your birthday is always a special day, and today is a spe-
cial birthday. Not only is it your "golden birthday," because
you are 13 on the 13th, it is the day you become a teenager,
the day everyone knows that you are well on your way to be-
coming an adult.

If I remember correctly, when one becomes a teenager, one
usually begins to wonder much more intensely "Who am I?"
and "How am I to live my life?" And if my experience holds
true for you, you'll be finding out who you are and discover-
ing how to live your life well into adulthood.

I think you are especially aware of what a gift life is because
your Dad's life ended too soon. And so I wonder if, as you ask
how to live your life—of yourself and of God—you ask with a
deeper passion than most people your age. Questions like
"Who am I?" and "What do I want to do with my life?" may
be particularly difficult because of your pain, but the pain also
contains the opportunity to find particularly rich answers.

Remember the letter Dad wrote you on your first birthday? He told you that you awakened us to great joy, and I believe that you continue to give him joy. A man who, on Earth, loved to show business associates the latest scrapbook of your photos even though it took up most of his briefcase surely now boasts about his boy in ways that astound his heavenly companions.

Which of Dad's values would he most like you to share? The first is faith. Your Dad's faith grew in his suffering, but I do not think he could have found such determination, strength, and peace in his suffering had the seeds of faith not grown in him throughout his life.

And I think your Dad would like you to inherit his optimism. He was drawn to heroes like Ernie Banks and Pete Gray (who, although he had only one arm, played outfield for the St. Louis Browns in 1945) because they were so positive, and he kept their pictures on the wall to inspire him. When your Dad was just out of college, he was a sales representative for Proctor and Gamble, and he had trouble selling one of his products, Duncan Hines muffin mixes (by the way, your Dad gave me a box of Duncan Hines blueberry muffin mix on our first date—but that's another story). You see, many of the ministers in Appalachia, where he was working, preached that the Proctor and Gamble trademark was of the devil. So your Dad baked some muffins for the ministers whom he visited. "I still didn't sell much muffin mix, but I met a lot of interesting people," he told me.

I hope that, like your Dad, you'll always look for the best in people. And if they disappoint you, learn how that has happened so that you won't be disappointed in yourself.

What would I like you to inherit from me? I'd also like you to inherit faith. There may be times, Ted, when you feel you have nowhere to turn except to God, and it's easier to find God when you already know that God is there.

I hope that when you see me up early in the mornings to write, when you see me at the computer (again) working on a sermon, when you see me e-mailing (there I am at the computer again!) to make arrangements for a vacation for the two of us, when you find the radio always set on classical stations, when you find it's hard to drag me away from a bookstore, when I want to drag you to the beach or museums or a play, that you will realize how much pleasure it gives me to follow my passions. How I hope to some day reenter my passion for the piano and to learn to paint, to indulge a new passion. As your passions emerge, I hope you will find ways to follow them. God has given us gifts to use for God, for others, and for ourselves, and we find and exercise those gifts in our passions. What do you make of your passion for dogs, for camping, for snowblading, for tennis and lacrosse (or will it be basketball, I wonder after I saw you play so well today, number 13!), for science, for music, even for The Simpsons? *What do those passions tell you about yourself? (Not that you asked me, but I think your passions reveal your curiosity, your sense of humor, your compassion, your sense of adventure, your creativity, and I like every single one of these things about you.)*

I hope that you'll find it easier to make friends with fear than I have. (When I see you snowblading or working on a skateboarding or rollerblading trick, I think you're off to a good start!) Thirty years older than you, I realize that most of my regrets were caused by fear. Why didn't I try to make it as an actress or make it otherwise in New York after I'd graduated from high school? Because I was afraid of New York. So when you find yourself deviating from your heart's desire, ask yourself if you're deviating from God's desire. If you don't think you are, then are you being held back by fear? I hope that you can give that fear to God and find courage in your trust.

And I hope that you will continue to fully engage yourself with your studies, because you will learn so much more that day. And the more you learn, the more you wonder, and the more you wonder, the more interesting the world is and the more choices you see for yourself. You have such potential as a student, Ted, and I imagine that sometimes it's difficult to live up to your potential. But when I see you working as well as you can, as I have especially this school year, the results are something in which you can—and do, I think—take great pride.

Mostly, Ted, I hope you'll realize that you were born of love—of the love of God and of the love of your Mom and Dad. And so, Ted, I hope you realize that you are invited to live in love, to live a life informed by love so you know that, in every decision you make and in every situation in which you live, there is love—the love of God and God's shadow of light: the light of those whom you love and who love you (count me in, please!), today, as well as in the past, the future, and in the life to come.

Love always,
Mom

Judy, an acquaintance of mine who works in a hospice-care setting, wrote these letters. She also wrote the following introduction
that provides a context for her ethical wills to her children.

It was December when I fit an MRI into an annual shopping
outing with a friend. Neither the neurologist nor I expected it to
explain my infrequent dizzy spells, but family history suggested
it was prudent. When I returned home from shopping, I had a
message to call the physician at home (an ominous request). I
was told I had a walnut size brain tumor pressing on my brain
stem. Although not likely malignant, it had to come out.

I had two weeks to put my life in order including some
overdue legal papers, tying up loose ends at work and keeping Christmas for my family. Although tasks kept me busy in
the daytime, my nights were consumed with fear.

Informed consent for the surgery included all that could
happen: paralysis, loss of speech and swallowing, blindness,
deafness, facial deformity or death. I made peace with the potential disabilities by rationalizing I'd deal with that when it
happened. Death was another matter. I was a 45-year old single mother of two teenagers. How could I leave my children?

The night before surgery in the hospital, after saying good-
bye to my children and visitors, I lay awake thinking of my
children and their futures. I felt compelled to write "only if"
letters. My available stationery was a school notebook. I borrowed two envelopes from a nurse.

Finishing the letters left me unexpectedly peaceful, a serenity that was still there in the morning when I was wheeled off
to surgery. With gratitude I can report I survived. After a few

weeks of rehabilitation I was able to return to my busy life. Several years later my children discovered the "only if" letters and asked to read them.

Dear Katie,

I write this not expecting that I will die, but in case something unexpected happens.

How can I tell you how important you have been to me—my first born, my only daughter, my quiet beauty.

I have so many special memories of our life together: both of us getting the giggles in church; our bright red twin rain coats when you were 3; being in the canoe wilderness with you (even when you didn't want to paddle); hearing you play Pachibel's Canon with the orchestra (even though you hated to practice); watching you comfort others like your teammate whose mother died; and buying you a prom dress a year early just because it was beautiful.

You are becoming a beautiful and self-reliant young woman. I am sorry we had to go through moments of distrust last year. I cherish growing close again this fall, even if it was a crisis on the eve of college that helped us to embrace.

Sex has not been an easy thing for us to talk about. It took me a long time to understand that it is a precious gift we can share with another human being, but it is best when love and trust are established first. Men, and some women too, can treat sex like recreation. I know you understand safe sex—please also keep looking for a loving, faithful relationship. Then you will have it all.

You will be a most wonderful teacher—I feel it whenever I see and hear you with children. Continue to take risks and reveal yourself to others. Then life will have a fullness you might not have believed possible.

Remember to give back to the earth. The lessons of the Boundary Waters and of Y Camp, to leave a campsite better than you found it, apply to decisions we make every day.

You have already discovered the joy of volunteerism with Habitat for Humanity, Camp du Nord, the North Dakota floods and your service sorority. Keep it as a lifelong habit to strengthen your core values by benefiting others.

Your dad is a good person who wants to be there for you. So do many others—Carol, Marcie, Sue, Susan and your friends. Cry with them, rage with them, or this grief can keep you from your dreams.

My love will always be with you—you get to keep it and remember it forever.

Love, Mom

Dear Brian,

I write to you tonight, not because I expect to die, but in case something unexpected happens.

You are so precious to me and many memories flood my mind. You were such a wanted baby—not to replace your brother who died, but because we believed in family and a son like you could fulfill that dream. I insisted on being awake for your surgical birth so I wouldn't miss a moment of your life with us.

I also remember you eating dog food (once or twice); sleeping on the bottom landing of the steps, reluctant to go to bed and miss anything; how you loved the sauna and jumping in the lake; how you loved to dress up and do theater; how well you sing; and your face when you opened the violin on Christmas morning when you were six.

I believe you can do anything you make up your mind to do. Practice does not come easy to you, but I see your pride when you put your creative efforts to work. I am a fellow procrastinator, but life is too tense that way. Try it a few times another way and you'll find unexpected peace.

For any ways we have struggled about weight control, I am truly sorry. My wish for you is optimum health so you can make your dreams come true. Dreams of high school, dating, marriage, children and maybe a career as a veterinarian. Your teacher Denise is a good confidant—she really loves you.

Remember to be good to the earth. You already love canoe camping and the Boundary Waters so you understand how to be a good steward of resources. Continue to embrace the causes and the behaviors that improve the environment.

Volunteerism is a value of mine which I hope you will continue: improving the lakes and rivers or the urban landscape, teaching reading or camping, feeding hungry people— whatever you decide. Your life will be enhanced even more than those you help.

I believe in you—how smart you are, how creative you are, how handsome you are, how honest and genuine and compassionate you are. Lots of people love you and can help you grieve. Don't run away from the pain and the grief—cry, write, draw, talk, and yell with people you trust.

I love you enormously—you get to keep and remember my love forever.

Love, Mom

This ethical will was written by a forty-seven-year-old father of two teenage daughters.

To my family:

In reading my ethical will, I hope that you find very few surprises. I believe I've been open about the things that I've valued over time. I've also tried to live my values on a day-to-day basis. I trust that I succeeded much more often than I've failed.

As I grew older (not that old!) and accumulated life experience (and life is a great teacher), I think I gained an appreciation of the importance of balance in my life. Balance among the family, work, spiritual, and physical aspects of life. And, having fun. It's easy to let things get out of balance. When they do, life can get out of control and become miserable. Always try to maintain a balance in your life.

Having a good sense of humor is very important. I know you've all moaned and groaned at my puns from time to time. Overall, the laughter was well worth it. It's important to have fun and there is humor in almost all aspects of life.

It's impossible to be successful in everything you try to do. So, don't be afraid of making mistakes. Just be sure you learn something from them. Sometimes you can learn more from a mistake than from always doing everything right.

Respect life—yours and others'. I'm a believer in the idea of treating other people the way you want to be treated. This is the proverbial "Golden Rule."

My hopes (for you, Alisha and Hannah) are that you find a vocation that adds value to the world. This is my interpretation of Tikkun Olam. I feel very lucky to have worked in the hospice world and devoting some of my energies to issues people face at the end of life. Trying to relieve suffering has been a worthwhile pursuit for me.

I hope you continue the traditions and faith of Judaism. Although this spiritual aspect of myself was relatively unimportant to me in my younger years, I feel you all have a wonderful foundation and excellent skills and knowledge in regard to the basic tenets of Judaism. I hope you will be able to pass these on to future generations.

I hope you are as lucky as I was in finding a soul-mate like your mother to share your life with; someone with whom to enjoy time together, grow together, solve problems together, face challenges together, support each other, and laugh and love together. It may not last forever, but the effort of staying together is worth it.

As I look back over my life, overall, I am happy with what I've accomplished. I've tried many things and would like to try some more. As long as you live you can always learn new things. This is an important value to cherish.

One of my regrets is that my parents and father-in-law weren't around to share in some of the things we (as a family) have done over the past 5–10 years. Another regret is not spending even more time together as a family. We certainly

112

*have taken some incredibly fun vacations: our three car trips
(to the west coast, Canada and Niagara Falls, Hershey-
Gettysburg-Washington DC-Williamsburg), Pinehurst, and
of course Italy. I'm glad we kept journals for all of them. You
kids just grow up so fast, and before you know it, you're out
there, (or soon will be) and on your own.*

*You all have been a great source of joy and strength for me.
I love you all very much.*

Dad

The author is a forty-seven-year-old wife and mother of four
children ranging in age from seventeen and almost off to college,
to four and still in pre-kindergarten.

She is a parenting columnist who often writes about her own
family life, so her children have lots of recorded memories of
their childhood, if they choose to read the columns when they
are grown. But she wanted to write an ethical will to filter a series
of conversations she and her husband have had over the years
about their families of origin, their own children's temperaments,
and the proclivities of their children's generation.

For my children, words to last a lifetime.

To my children:

*You have been the delight of my life, the crucible in which I
became an adult. I remember each of your births. They were
the most wonderful days of your parents' lives.*

*I know that my oldest child, Matt, probably wished some-
times he were the only child, and I have heard you two older
boys wonder aloud why we had the two smaller children. But*

four children made an absolutely right-sized family for your father and me.

Tom Cruise said to Renee Zellweger in the movie "Jerry Maguire," "You complete me." Well, each of you completed us and our family. I hope and pray that you will cherish and nourish your sibling ties as you grow up and grow old.

Because Dad and I are both wordsmiths and storytellers, the written word has always been important to us. Read as if your life depended on it; it does. Keep a diary; that way you can have a record of your childhood.

Keep in mind we have a family weakness for alcohol. You know that a couple of your uncles struggled to drag themselves out of the depths of alcoholism. Be suspicious of intoxicants. They are not the source of fun.

What is fun? Fun is running and shaking your booty. Fun is singing; fun is dancing to the music of the television commercials, as Maeve and Tom do. Fun is laughing, especially with those you love. Fun is sledding down Mr. MacPherson's hill, and going camping. Fun is being silly. Fun is discovering new things and new places, especially with those you love.

As I write this, there are reports that the Internet is starting to rob us of in-the-flesh personal connections. You can have fun on the Internet, but don't live and die by virtual fun. The most fun is face-to-face and touchable.

There's an old saying: "If it's worth doing, it's worth doing well." Let me amend that to say: "If it's worth doing, it's worth doing poorly." I fear that, more and more, your generation will shy away from taking risks, believing we have conquered the conquerable frontiers and that risks could endanger a comfortable status quo, a comfortable self-image.

But if you don't try, if you don't stretch, you don't develop. So try something you want to do that you've never done. And if you do it poorly in the beginning, keep at it. You'll do better. If it's worth doing, it's worth doing poorly. This message is aimed particularly at you, Matt. Don't always take the safe bet.

Freud, the old goat, said we are shaped by our work and our love. I believe that. We are also shaped by our whimsy and our passion and, God willing, they intersect with our love and our work. As I grow older, I also understand we are shaped by loss.

I am not especially church-oriented, but every day I say that line from the Scriptures: "This is the day the Lord has made: Let us rejoice and be glad."

I do believe we have a responsibility to the larger community. The trick is figuring out how to contribute. That's why Dad became a mentor to an urban kid. I tried to be helpful to readers and viewers who contacted me. We always contributed to charities we deemed worthwhile. I remember my mom sending small checks to Franciscan missionaries when I was a girl.

Dad and I used to disagree about whether a couple of our friends who died young had made a lasting contribution. "They frittered away their talent," Dad would say. And I would respond, "But maybe the purpose of their life was to pass a stranger on a street corner and give him a smile at a critical juncture."

Now you may think I'm being overly dramatic, but when I'm driving or walking outside, I make it a point to look at strangers, to nod, to smile. Maybe that's the purpose of my life. Always reserve enough leisure time and mental space to smile.

Through our work, your father and I have met rich people and celebrities. Wealth and high profile are their own challenges in life. I wish you enough money to support yourself, your family, and the good causes of your choice, and enough celebrity to get across the message you need to get across to those to whom you need to speak.

Matt, you seem to have a philosophical bent and good people skills. You say you want to be a psychologist. Tamp down any tendencies towards arrogance and let your native kindness and thoughtfulness guide the people in your care.

Mike, you are most like me in looks, temperament, sense of comedy, and writing ability. Try not to fight the similarities too much. You are like a razor cutting through bureaucracy, inefficiency, obfuscation, and hypocrisy. Hone your sharpness to get across your message. But try not to cut people out of your life with your razor-sharp wit.

Tom, you are such a sunny human being, the kind of 6-year-old who blows kisses to his mom through the kitchen window. Dad says you are most like him. Dad's advice to the adult you will become: "Treat every person you meet as no better or no worse than yourself. Treat everyone as exactly equal to you."

Maeve, you are the sole female of the siblings. I have no idea whether domestic responsibilities will be more evenly balanced between the sexes in marriages of your generation. At the age of nearly 5, you are already observant, self-sufficient, self-defining, both hearty and sensitive. I wish you the strength to become the very special individual you already are, while nurturing relationships, friends, and families.

One last thing: We have this family problem with joke-telling. Nanny always told the punch line first, and then backed her way down the buildup. One time, she gave the punch line "Wrecked 'em? Damned near killed 'em!" and then gave the buildup for a whole other joke. So always pre-play the buildup to the punch line in your mind before you tell a joke out loud. This joke-telling inadequacy may be a genetic thing.

No matter how lost or disconsolate you may seem at various points in your life, I hope this helps to bring you back on track: That your parents loved you intensely, unconditionally, and imaginatively. Remember my voice when I sang you "Tura, Lura" before you went to sleep.

Love, Mom

There are many similarities between an ethical will and a personal mission statement. The author of this document developed his personal mission statement over more than five years. It serves the same purpose as an ethical will although the style is less narrative than the previous examples.

My mission is to serve God by creating a balance between family, friends, profession, and community.

1. I will be guided by the teachings of Judaism.

2. I will act on situations and opportunities, rather than be acted upon.
3. I will not make assumptions of what people need. I will ask.
4. I will be a fair and honest evaluator of situations.
5. I will be positive. I will look for the good.
6. I will be courageous and persistent to experience and accept differences.
7. I will be sincere, yet decisive.
8. I will remember that one person **can** make a difference.
9. I will share. In sharing, one learns, experiences, and reaps the highest level of satisfaction.
10. I will keep a sense of humor.
11. I will not fear mistakes, for mistakes are the springboard of future success.

With family and friends, I will seek to understand first before being understood. I will be empathic, which is sympathy with a solution. Sometimes that solution is just to listen. I will be supportive and inspiring, attempting to assist those within my circle of influence to become interdependent people. My wife and children are my highest priority with regard to creating this positive interpersonal relationship.

Professionally, I will help people devise and implement financial and personal plans to afford these people financial and emotional independence. I will be honest and always put a client's best interest ahead of my financial reward. This is with the understanding that I must make an income to be able to service clients. I will only ask a client to do something that I do or hope to do once sufficient capital is acquired. The *best investment one can make is in oneself and other people. I will run a profitable business with equal emphasis on providing a positive work environment as well as profitability.*

To my community, I will allocate a minimum of 10% of my money and time. One area of focus will be in building bridges between Jews and non-Jews. My other area of focus will be with youth in 7th through 12th grade, helping to develop and implement programs that will help them to acquire the leadership skills necessary to become interdependent and effective adults.

My personal dreams today are:

1. *Have a meaningful and special relationship with my wife.*
2. *Raise responsible children.*
3. *Help people who demonstrate a caring for others, reach their goals.*
4. *Become a philanthropist.*
5. *Teach other financial planners this business.*
6. *Enjoy the people and the process.*

Additional notes:

1. *What is hateful to you do not do on to others.*
2. *Act as if all your actions will be part of a story published in the* Wall Street Journal.

Being a parent:
The goal of being a parent is to guide the child from ignorance to wisdom, from moral neutrality to virtue, from dependency to interdependence, from infancy to maturity. My

goal as a parent is to prepare the child to function as an independent adult in an interdependent society.

My obligation is to:

1. *Teach ethical and moral behavior*
2. *To have you wed*
3. *Teach you a craft (a means to make your own income)*
4. *Teach you to swim*
5. *Practice citizenship so that you may function as an upright and productive member of society*

This author was in her forties when she wrote this as part of a five-session seminar on "spiritual ethical wills."

For My Sons:

Thank you for allowing me to hold you in my body, in my arms and in my spirit for a short, precious time. Thank you for teaching me to be a parent and a better person, allowing me to grow through your growth. Thank you for your innocence that kept me from becoming jaded, gently urging me to look at the world differently, through your eyes. You helped me to see so much more. Thank you for your patience through my struggles to become the best I can be—best parent, best wife, best friend, best person.

Thank you for guiding me through the maze of inconsistency that was my constant nemesis, and reminding me of what is really important. You may have taught me more than I have taught you.

One of my greatest fears is that your memory will paint a portrait of me as a weak woman with good intentions, somewhere between a skilled housekeeper and a shrew, always "on your case." The thought horrifies me. Please remember me not only for what I did, or said, but for how I made you feel. Please remember that my desire to pass along what wisdom I may have gained from my experiences sprang from love, to ease your way and spare you pain, not a desire to control or make you a copy of me. Now THAT would be a nightmare!

I pray that some of my words found their way from my heart through sometimes deaf ears and a stubborn brain to your heart because that was where I tried to send them. My whole life of parenting I have struggled with an inner dichotomy of what is truly important.

My factual, living day to day self said that school was important, grades were important, as a key to unlocking whatever doors you wanted to open in your future. I tried to help you see that grades were more than so many superficial inkblots on a page—it was the knowledge behind those inkblots that would truly set you free to choose your own path.

The other side of the dichotomy was that part of me believed that none of this truly mattered, that life is more about how you treat people and how you feel about yourself, learning how to be gentle with your own shortcomings, while striving to become better. Following the path to change who you have been for who you want to become can be difficult in the beginning, filled with potholes and setbacks. Just remember to be gentle and loving with yourself along the way. What you first attempt to practice will become second nature in time. So celebrate your small steps in the beginning and know that everyone stumbles occasionally! And even though I may never come to terms with my dilemma, I pray that you might find that answer for yourself, in your lifetime.

I truly believe that each generation is meant to be wiser than the one before—an emotional, personal evolutionary process based on the experiences of those who have gone before, and the new generation's conscious choice to follow certain beliefs, depart from others, and explore new ones. My sincerest hope is that you will use the foundation we have tried to provide and then take off to build a structure that has never been imagined before—uniquely you—that will blow the world's socks off!

I will always love you both with all my heart and soul.

Love, Mom

The author of this ethical will was forty-seven when it was written. She was stricken with ALS (Lou Gehrig's disease). In addition to being unable to use her arms and legs, this woman also lost the use of her voice. She used a "light-board" for communication. This is a method where a light was attached to her head, and by her pointing to a letter board, words can be "written." This ethical will took two months to produce, and was basically done one sentence at a time at each social worker visit. The effort to produce even one sentence was exhausting, yet she insisted and persisted on creating her ethical will for her spouse and three children. She died about one week after finishing her ethical will. She remarked to the social worker who helped her through the process that writing her ethical will afforded her a sense of completion. Her family, receiving this very tangible legacy, enabled them to "let go." Her ethical will was read and displayed at her funeral.

Ethical Will of C. P.

The most important values that have guided me are:

SERENITY POEM

God grant me the serenity to accept the things I cannot change
The courage to change the things I can
And the wisdom to know the difference

THE TEN COMMANDMENTS

You shall have no other gods before Me
You shall not make idols or graven images or bow down to them nor worship them
You shall not make wrongful use of the name of the Lord your God
Remember the Sabbath day and keep it holy

Honor your father and your mother, so that you may live long in the land the Lord your God is giving you
You shall not murder
You shall not commit adultery
You shall not steal
You shall not bear false witness against your neighbor
You shall not covet your neighbor's house; you shall not covet your neighbor's wife, or male or female slave, or ox or donkey, or anything that belongs to your neighbor

Empathy
Walk in another person's shoes
Patience
Prepared October & November 1998

ETHICAL WILLS BY
AUTHORS IN THEIR FIFTIES

It was interesting, I have to tell you, talking with people like myself who had no children to leave a legacy for—how few of them believed they were "entitled" to write an ethical will. In some cases, they showed a bit of embarrassment, offering the old "Who would want to read my thoughts?" reason but from a decidedly disenfranchised place of being either single or childless. I myself felt it a bit but then charged ahead. I decided to mail my ethical will with my holiday letter this year, as much because I'm not sending a lot of presents as I am because, hell, I could be dead next year and I'd like to see what my loved ones think and how and if they respond.

To My Friends and Family,
Since I've never married or had children, I don't have a conventional family system, but I have definitely created my family of choice. I feel incredibly lucky to include in that my immediate blood family, but I also add into that number the amazing group of people whom I have been lucky enough to have love me. I often tell people that you are my greatest accomplishment. I have surrounded myself and bonded with the

most exceptional people I have ever met. Being part of a clan has always been vitally important to me, as many of you who knew me in my cult years know. I have not always made the wisest choices, but I believe that with your help I have milked my mistakes for whatever vast or minuscule lesson I could learn and then took it to heart. Through all this, I have tried to give you what I value most: honesty, trust, and unguarded love.

I think the need to learn has always driven me. I have tried to outgrow myself constantly. My spiritual beliefs might be hard for some to understand, but I believe that we are part of something incomprehensibly bigger than ourselves and that we are responsible to strive to understand it enough that we are able to give something back to this life we are blessed with. I have tried to treat each of you as though you have the potential to outgrow any obstacles or challenges you were given along the way, and if I have pushed you a little too hard because of that faith in you, I am sorry. The older I get, the more precious every moment is to me, and I want everyone I care about to live as large as they can.

Nature is alive to me, and I trust that it is absolutely complete in all the metaphoric instructions we need to know to live in our own divinity—God, hiding in plain sight, surrounding us every day. I wish for all of you, with your busy lives, to remember that all it takes is a good long walk in the woods several times a week to remember to listen to the smartest parts of yourself, the parts that will keep you in respectful relationship to your body, your life, and the universe.

Without kids, I've had to be more intentional in where I put my devotion and focus. My work with hospice has been *incredibly precious to me, as it has given me access to some of the language and experiences of letting go that we don't get growing up in this culture. I am grateful for what I've learned, and I hope that I have made a difference in the lives of the grieving people and coworkers whom I've been honored to work with. Having to remember to get myself out of the way to serve others has helped me overcome my natural tendency toward self-absorption. This is partly what I mean by "outgrowing myself." I've had the opportunity to be several, completely different people in this lifetime as I've shed each set of beliefs and limitations, and I recommend it to everyone.*

At 52, I have to say something to anyone who's younger than me. It's amazing to get older. Not necessarily fun, but amazing. Each age has its gifts and its limitations, and I hope that every young, middle-aged, and older person in my life gets the right kind of support to go for the gusto in their age-appropriate tasks. For example, I wish I'd finished my education when I was in my 20s and didn't have anything better to do. I did finish college in my late 40s, but it wasn't as easy as it would have been if I'd done it earlier. Your energy changes appropriately in each age. There's a lot more of it when you're younger, but it gets more sophisticated and interesting when you're older if you use it for the right things. I say this because I've had a hard time letting go of the past, generally. Today I'd tell anyone, don't miss a minute of your life by trying to hold on to something whose time is over.

My greatest life-transforming lessons have mostly come from my hardest times—working with a biochemical disorder, leaving the cult I was in while dealing with cervical cancer, the breakup of my serious relationships with lovers and friends. I think that's true of everyone—that you dissolve when you are in deep grief and you live in the possibility of deepening your values and focus. For me, as I said, they were lessons in letting go of the past, who I was and what I wanted, releasing my frantic need to never let go of anything. This must be one of my greatest lessons to learn in this lifetime, since I seem to be given opportunities to work with it almost daily.

Whatever difficulty presents itself to you is a gift, either something begging to be seen and understood, as Rilke said of our dragons, or a chance to let go of your personal agenda and align more with What Is. Same goes for whatever joy presents itself. Try to find your own way to trust God or the universe so that you can get a bigger picture than your own small agenda. Once you do, you realize how lonely you were.

Take care of your health. You're riding around in this in-credible vehicle with operating systems you can't even begin to grok [sic], and it's not only respectful to take care of it, it's critical if you're going to fully enjoy the ride. No matter what state your health is in, be grateful. There are lessons in illness, and the alternative to any state of health is death, so don't be complaining unless you're ready to get out of the vehicle.

I don't believe we are meant to understand ourselves, grow, grieve, change, or fully enjoy life without other sets of eyes that see us through love. If you can't let other people in, really in, to influence you and love you when you're at your worst, or save you sometimes, you are going to have a tiny little life and probably be very angry on your deathbed that you missed something and you don't know what it is. I pray for all of you that that never happens.

I've tried to be a good friend to all of you. I've tried to bring something into the world that may not have my name on it when I leave but that brought comfort, encouragement, and spark into people's lives. I meant what I said at the beginning of this letter: you are my greatest accomplishment and I'm so grateful that you have loved me.

Blessings, Kim

This ethical will is unique in that it was attached to the writer's Durable Power of Attorney for Health Care Decisions. The author of this will is a nurse by profession, and the mother of three children. Agewise, she's in her late fifties.

In the event that I cannot make my own health care decisions, there are no other people I trust more to make these decisions than the three of you. The three of you are growing into people I am proud to call my children and my friends. Each of you has different strengths and together you are a great team.

I am writing down a few of my wishes and values to guide you in the decisions if you have to make them. Being independent is a value that I hold very near and dear to my heart.

I remember as a small child hearing a consistent challenge from my father, one should always be prepared to care for themselves and be their own person. So much of what I am is because of Grandpa, and I dearly miss him every day. Each of you was lucky to have him in your life. And looking at how independent each child in his family has turned out, I think he is smiling at us each day (probably from a boat when he is out fishing).

If I am in a life-threatening situation where the outcome is most probably going to be a state of dependency, I do not want any extraordinary means employed to keep me alive. I do not want to be maintained on a respirator, receive artificial feedings, or have people resuscitate me if my heart stops. Death is not really the enemy, and I believe in another life after death. Death does not scare me, but living without any quality does. I like being a part of each of your lives and having a life of my own. Just being maintained with bodily systems is not my definition of living.

If I am paralyzed and cannot breathe on my own, if I have a critical head injury, if I suffer a large burn, if I have a significant neurological event, or require surgery that is only palliative, I want you to consider the outcome. What would be important to me is to be kept comfortable, free of pain, and have my family close by during my dying process.

These examples do not address every situation, they are just examples. Use your judgement. I trust you to make good choices.

If I am to die and can help another by donating organs, that is a practice I am in favor of. I would live on in each of you but just maybe in someone else also. However, if anyone of the three of you is opposed to this and does not feel comfortable, do not feel obligated to agree to donation. I have found this is a very private decision and makes some people uncomfortable.

I want my children to speak for my health care needs if I cannot. Please support them in these decisions, which they will make based on my values. I have seen people question decisions especially if they are not the decisions they would like made. Please don't do this. Health care decisions are hard to make and people do not need to be second-guessed.

I have a great life. I have three children I am proud of, an extended family that will be there for support, and a circle of friends that I cannot even begin to explain their importance. I have had fun and I see my life as an adventure. Humor ought to be a large part of every person's day. Every day there is a new mountain to climb. Some adventures are not much fun and do not turn out the way you want them to, but all of them shape who you are. I always make myself try to do new things because I swore never to get complacent and do only what is comfortable. This year I have made a decision that changed the makeup of our family, truly the most difficult decision I have ever made. Time will tell whether it is the right decision.

In the future I challenge the three of you to always be willing to climb new mountains and greet new adventures. I want to see a future where each of you is happy, that you make supportive and provocative mates if you marry, attentive parents who challenge any children that come, supportive family to your extended family, and a loyal friend to those you choose to call friends. Karen Kaiser Clark talks of growing deep not just tall. I heard her speak years ago, but I have never forgotten that statement.

The other concept that has guided me was in a book by Viktor Frankl. The concept emphasized what we can control in our lives. We cannot control so much that happens to or around us, but we can control how we choose to react to what happens to us. I cannot tell you how much this concept has helped me. It gives me a sense of control in situations even when I cannot control any of the events. And it helps me put events in perspective.

As I close here, I have to chuckle because I realize, even at the end of my life, I do not stop giving directions. Humor me, it is who I am.

Love, Mom

I missed my calling. Perhaps others "shoulda been a contenda." I "shoulda been a "teacha." There are several things I "shoulda" taught. One of them is what I call "life lessons"; not because my kids (or any one else's) need them but because I have gotten virtually every one of them wrong, and I desperately want to insure that others (my kids in particular) avoid the hurt I suffered from having done so.

In any event my kids were reluctant recipients of this accumulated wisdom. ("Oh Pop!!!!") But as they matured they learned to abide my "little idiosyncrasies"—see "rule" ten in the will. I had collected most of these sayings into my ethical will, but I was reluctant to do anything with it when, on September 18, 1998, my twenty-nine-year-old son, David, died. Writing about and to David (www.bigdave.org) helped the grieving process, and I determined to post the Will on the site that his friends had put together in his honor. He doesn't need it now—he's in heaven. But I just know that he's monitoring the site.

Whenever he reads it, I know it brings a smile to his face and an "Oh Pop" to his lips.

By the way, I wrote the Will not only for David but for Lisa, my absolutely wonderful daughter who I love with all my heart. (The hardest thing about David's death was to convince Lisa that I would have grieved just as heavily if she had died.) Ever the good daughter, she gave her approval to my posting the Will on www.bigdave.org and disseminating it more broadly.

On Rosh Hashanah, our rabbi talked about ethical wills, documents embodying the "life lessons" that you want to pass on to your kids. I had written such a document but had never gotten around to passing it on to David before he died. It finally occurred to me that David is not only in Heaven, but is monitoring this web site. So here it is, David, and as you read this, please remember item nine.

Ethical Will of Michael A. Greenspan

Michael Greenspan authored the following introduction and ethical will. He also created a Web site in honor of his deceased son, David. The Web address is contained in Mike's introduction.

Having disposed of my property through duly executed documents, I now turn to the harder job of leaving to my children, Lisa and David, a set of principles that they should consider in living their own lives and in helping to shape the lives of their children.

1. *Do the right thing—as often as you can.*
2. *Only worry about those things that you can do something about.*
3. *Try as hard as you can, and, having done so, don't look back if things don't work out.*

4. *Work hard, but stop before you mindlessly begin work to ask whether you have found the most efficient thing to work hard at.*

5. *You are not the center of the universe. If it takes religion to make you realize that, then embrace religion.*

6. *Happiness is NOT what feels good at the moment. You also have to consider the long-term consequences of your actions.*

7. *Be positive; try to find the best in a bad situation.*

8. *Be interested in a lot of things. People who are interested are interesting.*

9. *Show everyone that you love that you love him or her, and be sure to tell him or her as well.*

10. *Divide the world into two groups: those that are trying to hurt you and those that aren't. Fight the first group as hard as you can and cut the second group as much slack as you can.*

11. *In making decisions, tend toward those that maximize your options.*

12. *Procrastinating over a decision until there is no decision to be made is itself a decision.*

13. *The best trait, in a friend, co-worker, or yourself, is dependability. The second is loyalty.*

14. *If you find a good, true friend, hold on to him or her as hard as you can.*

15. *Ask not what people do, but how well they do it.*

16. *Be fruitful and multiply.*

17. *And three that I have heard before but really like:*
    (a) When things are going REALLY wrong, remember: that which doesn't kill you makes you stronger,

(b) Love like you've never been hurt before, and
(c) Dance like no one's watching.

This author was the mother of four children and grand-mother of five. She was in her early fifties at the time of her death. She hand wrote copies of this will to all of her children on stationery that she designed herself. Her favorite TV show was *All My Children* so she provided this title to her ethical will.

To All My Children
My dear children:
You must know by now how very much I love each and every one of you. In happy times and tough times we have al-ways supported each other as a family. My wish is for each of you to accomplish something in life. Follow your dreams, never give up, and be happy along the way.

I have made mistakes, nobody is perfect, but I always had your best interest in mind, and always did the best I could to the best of my ability.

God has blessed me with beautiful, loving, good-hearted children. I feel your love every day and that gives me strength. I also want to express my love and say thanks to my sons-in-law, "RK" and "R," and my daughters-in-law, "T" and "D," for their support and care. To my beautiful, sweet grandchildren "S," "B," "J," "C," and "B," who give special meaning to my life. Their innocence and the love they give me so freely fills my heart with happiness. When I watch all of you with your children, I feel so proud to see how much you love them and they love you in return.

Forgiveness, compassion, love, responsibility, and hope, are all-important words in my book. I hope that someday you can all get closer to your father. We all need to be loved and feel needed.

I have always been there for you and will continue to do so, to advise you, if you ask, or just to listen.

Life is full of memories and I have had my share of them. Try to remember and hold on to all the good memories we have shared together.

I also have some regrets, but who doesn't. Life is not always fair. Sometimes we just accept what we cannot change. Forgive me if I have hurt you in any way or if I have been too hard on you at times. Just remember, a mother's love is true and endless.

Try to find joy and beauty in the simple, ordinary things that life has to offer. Time is precious, do not waste it or take it for granted.

I love you all forever,
Mom

Ethical Will by Don Schmitz

February 12, 2001
Dear Jeff, Andrew and Ted and Grandchildren;

Purpose

It is my hope in writing my ethical will that I will be able to record for posterity some of my values and visions for the future. I hope this will help each of you as you plan and carry out your life. In my studies of leaving a legacy, I was re-minded how important it is for parents and grandparents to share and record what is important to them. For posterity's sake, I have attempted to record some of my experiences and what I believe in, some history of what I have done with my life, and lessons I have learned along the way.

Introduction

I want you, my family, to know how important you all are in my life and how much I love you. A better life for you than what we had was always our goal. Sometimes, as a parent, we tried to protect you from falls and hurts. These hurts occurred throughout life; from the time you first started to walk, or ride around the block on your big wheels, to bicycles and finally cars. At the same time, your mother and I wanted you to be independent and stand up for yourself when obstacles would get in your way. There was never anything in our lives that equaled having the three of you for our sons (yes not even the grandchildren, though they sure are nice too!). We've always wanted the best for each of you and helped you as much as we possibly could. How proud I have always been to have you for my sons!

A. SOME OF MY EXPERIENCES

My Trip to See Mary Reuvers

One of the experiences I remember as a little boy was when I went to see Mary Reuvers. We were never allowed to go anywhere without getting permission from our parents. This

Taffy and the Fair

Another childhood story I recall was taking my calf, Taffy, to the Rice County Fair. Taffy was about six months old when we started her training. We later learned that at six months, she was already too old to be trained effectively to take to the fair but we didn't know it at the time.

Taffy had a lot of spunk, but Dad always referred to it as "stubbornness." Taffy never learned to walk around with me using a halter but instead she dragged me around but I persisted each day trying to get her to walk with her halter by my side.

Bill, my brother, also took a calf to the fair. Her name was Tuffy. She was a much more mild-mannered calf and easier to train. It was a real big thing that we were given this opportunity because it took a lot of time away from the chores and yet for some reason Dad allowed it. As I look back on this, it's still a real surprise.

Soon it was time for the fair and Bill's calf got a blue ribbon but mine got a red. I was so disappointed but excited at the same time because I got invited to take Taffy back to another show the next day. I remember Dad talking to me that night and that he would even come and watch me in the ring!

The next day was a disaster! As soon as I got Taffy into the show ring she got scared and ran away. I felt like such a failure especially with my dad being there.

We were never allowed to take calves to the fair again. As hard as this experience was I learned a lot about life. I learned how difficult life can sometimes be and that you don't always get everything you want in life even if you work hard. Today, that is still one of my characteristics, extremely persistent.

Marbles

When I was about eight years old I remember playing marbles at school. Mom made me a bag out of scraps with a drawstring at the top, I was so proud of it.

Someone had determined that "Cat's Eyes and Steelies" were the most valuable marbles. Bill and I discovered that Steelies were nothing more than ball bearings.

One day we took apart some old machinery and found a couple really big "steelys" to use as shooters. I remember how excited I was going to school and how long school was that morning until recess. That day, I won all kinds of marbles from Jim Walsh and Tom Merrill, two of my classmates. When I came home with all the marbles Bill and mom couldn't believe it. Oh how proud I was of myself.

B. THINGS THAT I VALUE

Your mother, Mary, was also someone I valued a great deal in my life. She is a very good person. Unfortunately, we were unable to stay married but that doesn't diminish her value.

Mary and I met in Mankato when she was nineteen and I was twenty. We were wild about each other from the very start. I remember how cute she was and what a gorgeous smile she had. We shared many wonderful and some rocky times over the years. Marriage is not an easy thing but persistence kept us together for 33 years.

Another thing that helped keep us together was prayer. Prayer can be extremely powerful. You don't always get everything you pray for and sometimes it takes a lifetime to know why God never let us stay together. As of this writing, I still don't know.

Counseling helped but nothing could ever stop the snowball of fate that hit us over time. In marriage you both don't grow at the same time. Sometimes you need to wait for your partner to grow through a stage and other times he or she will need to wait for you, but you also need to be your own person and live your own life.

The following are some of the highlights I am most proud of in my life:

Getting my college degree
Having a strong faith
Having Mary and Leo Marso as my mother and father in law, they were very special people. Sometimes, I believe I loved Mary's parents more than my own.
Having the three of you early in our marriage
Teaching school for twenty years
Being chosen "Teacher of the Year in 1984"
Getting my Masters and Specialist Degree in Education
Owning our three homes in Cottage Grove and our mansion at 285 Summit
Being your basketball coach
Reading books to all of you
Teaching you our faith
Being friendly to all we come in contact with

Involvement in the community; Chambers, Teaching Organizations and the Youth Service Bureau

St. Rita's Church (Co-Chair of the building expansion committee for our church)

Chosen "Citizen of the Year" by the Cottage Grove Chamber of Commerce in 1994

Receiving the Youth Service Bureau Award in 1999

My ten years with Jeane Thorne and the part I played in the growing Jeane Thorne

Buying and rebuilding our mansion at 285 Summit in St. Paul

Our three grandchildren

Learning to play the guitar

Having built a strong financial background for the future

Working on another degree in Human Development from St. Mary's

C. THINGS I BELIEVE IN

Strong families and the need to stay together: As I've grown older I continue to value my children and grandchildren more and more. I enjoyed my study of the Genealogy of our family. It's my hope that someone will continue my work and maintain our family information in the years to come.

The power of education: How important it was for your Mom and me to help you get college degrees. We were always so proud of your educational accomplishments. I believe that the dollars we spent on your education was some of the best money we spent.

Parents should read to their children: I remember how special it was for me to be able to hold you on my lap and read to you. As a former first grade teacher, teaching you to read was so special. The three of you have all grown to be better readers and writers than I am and I know that it's been a valuable part of our growing up.

Follow your heart: People must follow their heart in what they want out of life. Money comes in handy too, but in the end your heart will benefit you the most. Too much money gives you too many choices, choices you often don't need.

Helping the poor: We have a responsibility to help others who are less fortunate. Giving money to the poor and to your church gives you a great feeling but it also hurts.

Taking time to smell the roses: One of the keys to raising a wonderful family was taking family vacations. We saved and saved our money and financially it was always difficult, but the experiences we shared were never forgotten. I especially remember our vacation to Washington DC, our trip to California, our eventful car ride through Sweden when Jeff was getting married, our many trips to Disney and our meals at the cabin.

Ongoing education throughout life: We can never allow ourselves to stop growing. The world is so big and there is so much to see and do. The more we continue to grow the healthier our brain is as we grow older. It will keep you young!

Respecting our land: I have been so lucky to be raised in this beautiful country. Respect of the land and its beauty is one of our responsibilities. I love flowers and plants and golf courses for their beauty. This is one area where man has been able to improve the beauty of the earth. I remember seeing the area around Orlando before Walt Disney developed the property and what it looked like after. God wants us to beautify his earth, if he didn't, he would have made it so we couldn't change the earth.

Raising children: I believe children should be brought up with a strong faith. I have found over the years that a strong faith is something that will stand the test of time. As you grow, you may choose to change your faith, but having a strong faith as a child can never be replicated.

A strong healthy body: I believe in exercise and eating carefully and caring for the only body we have. It's also important to get annual examinations and getting proper rest and good exercise. Healthy bodies will improve our life expectancy and the quality of life as well.

A life of your own: I also believe in taking time for yourself. My trips to Canada for fishing always left me more thankful for the life I had and the people in it. A good movie or book can provide a real welcome break as well. Daily walks, journaling and meditation are other ways I have practiced to better appreciate the simple things around you.

D. LESSONS I HAVE LEARNED

Everyone must live their own life in their own way, as their values would have them live. Any variation of this is just a short-term diversion. Telling others how to live their life is not in anyone's job description.

People do change. I've seen many wonderful changes made by people who are willing to continue to grow.

Finding a career you are proud of is very difficult but worth the search. You may need to try many different careers during your life. Don't be afraid of change. Fear is lack of experience and the only way to conquer it is to do it! I've had many wonderful careers; farming, student, teacher, businessperson and business owner.

Computers are a lot like us. Sometimes I think we are a lot like a computer. Every once in a while we need to get rid of the old computer and start new. No matter how much you tweak the old one, it is still old. Opal used to say; "I wish we had a Delete button so we could do a better job of forgiving and forgetting." Maybe computers have some advantages over people!

Raising children while you are still young: Have your children when you are young. Children are very exhausting and can best be handled when you are young.

Keep listening. You learn nothing while you are talking.

When raising your children, don't worry about all the little stuff. It's not what people say that matters; it's what they do. Love your children; let them know you love them unconditionally and pray, pray a lot!

Be thankful for all the gifts of life. Life isn't fair and each of you has different gifts. God knew what he was doing and who are we to question him?

E. Things That Had
a Big Impact on My Life

Mary Marso, your grandmother, was a very special lady who helped me greatly to believe in myself and to believe in the value of prayer. She loved me unconditionally. I hope you can

*say that about us. It was her belief and prayer for me that got
me through college. I couldn't have done it without her.*

*Sr. Michelle was my American History teacher at Bethle-
hem Academy. She always believed in me and encouraged me
to make the most of myself.*

*Being chosen "Teacher of the year" in Cottage Grove was a
wonderful thing for me. It was one of the most important
awards in my life. Take the time to recognize other special
people in the world. There are far more awards that should be
given, that never are. I encourage you to make it your business to give lots of awards in life, both formal and informal.*

*The death of Mary's parents at such a young age had a
tremendous influence on Mary and a large influence on me
as well. They were such good people who always gave time
to anyone in need. They are good examples for you to follow.
Your grandmother expected a lot of her children and her
children worked hard to live up to her expectations. What
does that say for you and your children?*

*Being the father of three wonderful boys was one of the
most special things in my life. I miss all of you even now
when I write this. Your mother and I spent so much time en-
joying all of you and we still do. One regret is not having all
of you closer, geographically, so I could drop by to see you
(and you to me). I always wished I could have helped you
more and just "be" with you.*

*I especially enjoyed our fishing trips together in Canada
and teaching you how to fish.*

F. WISHES FOR THE FUTURE

You will each find a mate that will love you, be the mother of your children and grow with you throughout your life.

I hope that my new career working with grandparents is successful. I've spent a great deal of time preparing for it and believe it will benefit many people.

I hope you get the chance to have children of your own and to experience the love they can bring into your life. I also hope you get to know your grandchildren and share with them your legacy and heritage. Families are so important!

Respect your time alone. You need your own time and space. Be supportive of yourself and your own ideas. Take time to nurture them and develop them to the fullest. Always remember that I am here and we will always be here in mind or in body to support you every step of the way; once a parent always a parent.

I hope we will be able to live into our 80's and beyond. There are so many stages of life, each brings its challenges and joys and no one can live it for you.

I hope I can stay healthy and be able to travel to visit you wherever you are.

I also hope I will be able to help you financially and that you give your children every opportunity to grow and learn. You can't do it for them.

Last I pray that you will be happy. Happiness is sometimes very elusive and ever changing but something that no matter what age we continue to seek. Remember that I love you and have done everything I could to raise the three of you and all the grandchildren as best I could.

Love your mates and pray that they will continue to love you. As Forrest Gump said, "Life is a bowl full of chocolates."

G. CONCLUSION

Thank you for your continued love and for being my children and grandchildren. I loved being your father and grandfather.

I love you very much and unconditionally will continue to love you as long as I live no matter what may change in our future.

You have been a great source of joy and strength.

Thank you for being my heirs.

Love,

Dad and Grandfather

This will was written in the earlier part of the twentieth century. It has a very interesting history.

In the pocket of an old ragged coat belonging to one of the insane patients at a Chicago poorhouse, a will was found after his death. According to Barbara Boyd, in the *Washington Law Reporter,* the man had been a lawyer, and the will was written in a firm clear hand on a few scraps of paper. So unusual was it, that it was sent to another attorney; and so impressed was he with its contents, that he read it before the Chicago Bar Association, and a resolution was passed ordering it probated. It is now in the records of Cook County, Illinois.

I, Charles Lounsberry, being of sound and disposing mind and memory, do hereby make and publish this my Last Will and Testament, in order, as justly as may be, to distribute my interests in the world among succeeding men.

That part of my interests which is known in law and recognized in the sheep-bound volumes as my property, being inconsiderable and of no account, I make no disposition of in this, my Will. My right to live, being but a life estate, is not at my disposal, but, these things excepted, all else in the world I now proceed to devise and bequeath.

ITEM: I give to good fathers and mothers, in trust to their children, all good little words of praise and encouragement, and all quaint pet names and endearments; and I charge said parents to use them justly, but generously, as the deeds of their children shall require.

ITEM: I leave to children inclusively, but only for the term of their childhood, all, and every, the flowers of the field, and the blossoms of the woods, with the right to play among them freely according to the custom of children, warning them at the same time against the thistles and the thorns. And I devise to the children the banks of the brooks and the golden sands beneath the waters thereof, and the odors of the willows that dip therein, and the white clouds that float high over the giant trees. And I leave the children the long, long days to be merry in a thousand ways, and the night and the moon and the train of the Milky Way to wonder at, but subject, nevertheless, to the rights hereinafter given to lovers.

*ITEM: I devise to boys jointly all the idle fields and com-
mons where ball may be played, all pleasant waters where
one may swim, all snow-clad hills where one may coast, and
all streams and ponds where one may fish, or where, when
grim winter comes, one may skate, to have and to hold the
same for the period of their boyhood. And all meadows, with
the clover-blossoms and butterflies thereof; the woods with
their appurtenances; the squirrels and birds and echoes and
strange noises, and all distant places, which may be visited,
together with the adventures there to be found. And I give to
said boys, each his own place at the fireside at night, with all
pictures that may be seen in the burning wood, to enjoy without hindrance and without any encumbrance of care.*

*ITEM: To lovers, I devise their imaginary world, with
whatever they may need, as the stars of the sky, the red roses
by the wall, the bloom of the hawthorn, the sweet strains of
music, and aught else they may desire to figure to each other
the lastingness and beauty of their love.*

*ITEM: To young men jointly, I devise and bequeath all
boisterous inspiring sports of rivalry, and I give to them the
disdain of weakness and undaunted confidence in their own
strength. Though they are rude, I leave them to the powers to
make lasting friendships, and of possessing companions, and
to them exclusively I give all merry songs and brave choruses
to sing with lusty voices.*

*ITEM: And to those who are no longer children, or youths,
or lovers, I leave memory, and bequeath to them the volumes
of the poems of Burns and Shakespeare, and of other poets, if*

there be any, to the end that they may live the old days over
again, freely and fully without tithe or diminution.

ITEM: To the loved ones with snowy crowns, I bequeath
the happiness of old age, the love and gratitude of their chil-
dren until they fall asleep.

ETHICAL WILLS BY
AUTHORS IN THEIR SIXTIES

Ray wrote his ethical will when he was sixty-six years old. It
was written as part of an assignment as he was learning to become an ethical wills workshop facilitator.

12/29/1938 – _____ What I have learned so far on
the dash

Dear Michelle, Dan, and my dearest Stephanie,

First of all I want you to know how important all of you
are in my life journey and how much I love you. It was sel-
dom that my full-blooded Irish father said the words "I love
you," but we never doubted it for an instant. I am sorry that
you, Michelle (Mik) and Dan (Daniel Patrick Joseph Paul)
never knew your Irish Grandpa, but your good humor and
hard work carry on his spirit, and the gleam in his eye is
there in each of yours. I have tried hard to be a conduit to
you from him. Of course your French Grandpa Turgeon
knew you, Michelle. I wish he had known you better, Dan,
since you were only two when he died. I am so glad that he
permitted this Irishman to marry his only daughter.

Education has been very important to me throughout my life so far. My mother and dad nurtured that love of learning. They taught me that it is not so much degrees or certificates as it is about being better prepared to serve people's needs more efficiently and effectively. I can see that you have both learned that well. Michelle, as I told you before, you are a great mother to Emily and her brother yet to be born. I'm sure you absorbed much of that mother love and dedication from your mom, who did such a good job as mother to you and Dan. The magic and love that you and Bob have for each other is certainly a huge factor in your parenting. Bob has always been just like a big brother to Dan, and I am so proud that he is part of our family.

Travel has always been a top priority with me. Seeing new places and the amazing variety of God's creation has been a fun ride. I like the challenges of imagining what to do, from camping and biking across Canada to visiting most of the Western states. I usually come up with the "great ideas," and you, Stephanie, the practical one, helped us know how to do it. I hope you continue to remember the good times we had and still do. Sometimes it is just a great trip downtown on the light rail or a quick canoe ride, swim, and picnic at Cedar Lake. Those "mini-vacations" always replenish my spirit, and my hope is that they will continue to do that for you too. Sometimes I have found that the short, simple travels are easy and unencumbered.

I am still working hard, and probably will for the rest of my dash, on being able and willing to ask for help. You are always there, Stephanie, and often anticipate most every need of the three of us. In recent times we have learned the power of the prayer of Jabez, and God has indeed blessed us, enlarged our territory (and our family). I am so glad that God protects and supports us daily.

One last thought from me through the words of Father Mychal Judge, who died in the 9/11 debacle: "Lord, take me where you want me to go, let me meet who you want me to meet, tell me what you want me to say, and keep me out of your way." My hope for you is that you would join me in asking God to bless your days as you live the rest of your dash in the spirit of Mychal's prayer.

I love all of you with all my heart and soul. I pray that all of us continue to have health, happiness and prosperity and generously contribute to the lives and welfare of those we meet.

Dad(dy) and Lover

This is an ethical will written by a widowed mother and grandmother. She is in her early sixties.

To My Children and Grandchildren:

MY FAMILY

The foundation of my life was laid by my wonderful parents who made me feel loved, competent, and confident. They taught me the central importance of family relationships—my father through his life-long study of family history and his collections of letters, stories, and family trees; my mother through her maintenance of personal connections with relatives scattered around the world. The love I share with my brother and sister and their families continues to be a cornerstone of my security. I learned at home that love cannot be required, even among relatives, but that caring and respect ought to be.

I had a special relationship with my grandmother. She lived next door to us and taught modesty, moderation and strength by personal example. From her I learned that one should "do good for the sake of good, not for the sake of reward" and that "there is no end of good that can be done by those who don't care who gets the credit."

JUDAISM

From my family I learned that it is important to know your own background: Of which tree are you a branch? In which chain are you a link?

For us, Judaism is the chain of connection. I believe it remains the best one for us, although other religions and value systems work well for other people. For me, the appeal of Judaism centers on the intellectual challenges it offers. It specializes in questions without answers and acknowledges the weaknesses and limitations of human beings while encouraging them to achieve their highest potential.

For me, Judaism (especially my membership in Vassar Temple) has provided a social context for relationships with others who have a common link but enough differences to make them interesting. I have also found the customs of our tradition, combined with the personal freedom of the Reform approach, to be psychologically sound.

I have not found a unifying purpose for life but I believe that each of us can make each day important and meaningful to ourselves. His philosophy gives each of us a lot of personal responsibility. I believe that the only eternal life over which we have control is our remembrance of those we love who have died.

LEARNING AND KNOWLEDGE

These two keep us mentally sharp, keep us open to growth and change, enable us to contribute professionally and personally, and can provide us with pleasant hours. I believe, as my mother did, that hard work and intelligence can go far to overcoming many problems.

It is a privilege to be able to share your knowledge and your love of learning with others. I have been fortunate to find many opportunities for teaching, both formal and informal.

TAKING AND GIVING

In giving you make your life worthwhile. But if you don't take, you will have nothing to give. Don't refuse to accept: others need a chance to give also.

I hope you will make the world a better place, both on a smaller scale and in the wider sense. Try to be a part of the solution, not part of the problem. Keep before you for inspiration a vision of the way things ought to be and help us move, albeit so slightly, in that direction.

APPRECIATION AND LOVE

My life has been enriched by an appreciation of nature. I hope you too will notice its variety and allow nature to refresh you.

Do not take for granted your physical and mental health and strength when you have it, nor lose hope when you don't.

My life has been enriched by wonderful friendships but the love of my family has been the most precious gift I have. Your father and grandfather offered me a love and a life which I always feared was too good to last. My love for him will never die. I picture the world to come as the opportunity to relax again in his arms.

My children, you are sources of joy and pride. You make me feel loved and cared for. Your thoughtfulness is touching and our interactions are a pleasure for me.

My love for my grandchildren is too great to express in words. I hope I have expressed it in other ways. Your existence gives me hope for the future and our mutual love gives me the greatest happiness.

ETHICAL WILLS BY
AUTHORS IN THEIR SEVENTIES

This ethical will was written by a man in his early seventies. He was diagnosed with lung cancer about six months earlier. He didn't have much time left when he composed this ethical will with the help of our hospice chaplain.

Dear Family and Friends,
The following are the things that I have learned through life:
Never give up.

Through having cancer, I have learned that one can't always believe the doctor, who at one time only gave me three weeks to live. Keep fighting it, keep doing it, and be stubborn, but be open to other people.

Faith in God is important.

I don't know why I'm still here. I am not all that religious, but I am a believer. I have learned how to say no. One can't do everything. Never be afraid to say, "I'm sorry, please forgive me." Ask for God's forgiveness.

Recovery is important.

Through recovery, I have gotten through a lot. My recovery is following the AA program, especially the serenity prayer. I've learned to listen to other people's stories. (Mine isn't the worst, believe me.) I've had 23 years of sobriety since 10/21/75.

Learn to be humble.

I've learned to be as honest as you can be. If you want something, for God's sake, ask for it. You can't read minds. The "wisdom to know the difference" comes from God. Be the best person you can be. This may mean to do the simple things like have a fire pit, and roast hot-dogs and marshmallows.

Be generous with love.

Through my mother and a neighbor named Gus, I've learned to have a good sense of humor. Learn to live day by day and have acceptance of another's quirkiness. Have a willingness to be open.

My hopes for my family and friends:

I hope that everyone can learn to get along. Whatever will happen will happen; one must learn to accept that and not control it. Forgive whatever misunderstandings or differences there are. Not all people can be the same. I hope, especially for my family, to get along in life and make a living for themselves. I hope that all can believe in God. I hope that you can remember the good memories, such as going on the camping trips.

A special note to my seven kids:

Each one of you is so different. You wouldn't know that you were related except for your looks. But you all have a little bit of me hanging around you, some good, and some not so good.

Finally, I am thankful for all those who have been good to me and have been helpful. I've learned to live a good life. I hope a good life for all.

Good-bye.

This is the ethical will written by my father about a month before he died. It also appears in Chapter 2. I wasn't consciously aware that I asked my father to write an ethical will at the time; I realized several years later that my request for a "letter" from him was a request for his ethical will. I later learned that he wrote additional personal letters to his older brother (who helped raise him after their mother died when my dad was nine years old), to several nieces and nephews, and to my brother.

This letter remains one of the most cherished remembrances I have of my dad.

Dear Barry and Sandy:

A few words to express my feelings and thoughts while time is running out on me. Some standard values I have lived by throughout my life are that I have always believed in honesty and advocated truthfulness.

I cherish the family with all my heart. I always felt I gave of myself to each of you. The satisfaction and gratification I received in return is in the accomplishments of my children. No father could be as proud as your father is of you. You have more than exceeded my greatest expectations. You continue to move forward in a manner that makes me love you more and more. I'm proud to say, "that's my son!"

Through the years, I've tried to take care of my family and provide some of the better things in life. I tried and succeeded in being able to give my children a good education. Although I was only a working man, many were the times I worked two jobs for the extra money so the family could have a little bit more. I had often thought of going into some kind of business, but didn't have the expertise in any particular field, or the finances to afford the luxury of risk. I'm proud to say that you have shown me through the years, the aggressiveness that I lacked emerged in you.

I have tried to be financially sound and leave behind an adequate amount of finances to carry your mother through the rest of her days. Since no one can predict the future, I ask that should it ever be necessary, see that your mother remains comfortable financially and otherwise.

Sandy, you have always made me proud with your accomplishments and different endeavors. You have never undertaken a task that was under-achieved. Through the years you have been in my confidence and as close as a daughter. You are a good wife and excellent mother. Barry could not have picked a finer mate.

My concentration is not too great at this point, as I'm sure I can say much more.

I hope [your daughters] Alisha and Hannah follow in the footsteps of the family. I love you all.

Dad

Ethical Wills by Authors in Their Eighties

The author of this ethical will, Mr. William Bell of St. Joseph, Missouri, is a widower who will be celebrating his 80th birthday next month. He said it was fine to say he was already eighty. In December 1999, he was asked if he would consider creating an ethical will for a newspaper story by a friend and reporter for the *St. Joseph News-Press*. He was given an *Ethical Will Resource Kit*, and six to eight weeks later, the following finished product was delivered. Since completing his ethical will, Mr. Bell plans to write much more about his family history, and publish it as a book for his family.

Ethical Will of Bill Bell

To my dearest family,

As I think about my life, I need to tell you about some of the experiences that have occurred in my life. There are many events that have happened to me and to our family. I wish to recount them for you so that you may see how they have shaped my personal beliefs, especially my belief in the importance of education.

I will be 80 years old in April. My wife, Molly, and I were married in September 1944 and lived together for over 52 years. She passed away in November 1996. We were raised in different areas of the country and met in early stages of World War II in her hometown, here in St. Joseph. Molly was starting her career at the St. Joseph News-Press. *I was a pilot in the U.S. Air Force.*

My duties in the Air Force involved a foreign tour of duty of 18 months, and when I returned to the United States I was stationed again at Rosecrans Field, here in St. Joseph, in April 1944. I was discharged from the Air Force in October 1945, and we moved to Houston, Texas. I returned to my pre-war employer McKesson & Robins, a wholesale pharmaceutical company.

Two of our children, Alice and Randy, were born in Houston. We moved back to St. Joseph on Jan. 1, 1950, and I became a partner in a car-rental business with Molly's brother, Jarrot McCord. Molly soon returned to work at the News-Press. *We then purchased a home at 2215 N. 22nd St. in 1952. This home was only a few blocks from Eugene Field grade school and our children were able to walk back and forth to school. This was a very important part of our lives.*

Alice entered Eugene Field School in the fall of 1952, and our son, Sam, was born in 1953. Randy entered Eugene Field School in 1956. Another daughter, Amy, was born in 1956.

I was employed by the CD Smith Drug Co. as assistant sales manager in January 1959. I worked there for a little over 32 years.

Katie, our youngest daughter, was born in 1965 and followed our other children in starting her education at Eugene Field. After attending Eugene Field School, all of our children entered Central High School. We felt at this point in our lives that a good education program for them was very important, and Central certainly offered that.

In their sophomore year at Central High School, each of the children began to go to their counselor and check out colleges where scholarships were available for their continuing education. With a mixture of scholarships and part-time jobs they were all admitted to colleges and completed their four years on schedule.

Alice went to Wellesley College in Massachusetts. Randy went to Westminster College in Missouri. Sam went to Washington & Lee University in Virginia. Amy went to Lawrence University in Wisconsin. Katie went to Washington & Jefferson College in Pennsylvania.

These were all reasonably small schools with excellent educational standards. Four of the five children went on to graduate studies. Their education led each of them into different occupations. They are very successful in the fields of law, computer software, finance, geology and natural resources, hospital business and administration.

Proper education is a very important need in our world. But the need, value and acceptance of this changes continually. For instance, our perception of the level of education needed in the

1940s—when I was coming of age—has changed from the 1950s as it has from the '60s, '70s, '80s and on.

Molly and I were very pleased that our children entered Central High School. The St. Joseph school system was a big help in counseling them about how, when and where to further their learning. As a family, their success with careers has fulfilled our hopes for them.

It is gratifying to know that this same planning is being accomplished with their children. Education does not stop or even slow down upon reaching a certain level; it continues all of our lives.

ETHICAL WILLS BY
AUTHORS IN THEIR HUNDREDS

My Ethical Will

My name is Beatrice Taishoff, and as I approach my 100th year, I am, to the best of my knowledge, the only living member of my generation. I would like to be remembered long after I am gone from this world for how I was able to cope with circumstances of life, which made me a stronger person. I do not believe it could have been possible in any other country than the United States of America.

As I write this, I have been residing for three months in the Jewish Home and Hospital in the Bronx section of New York. I was born on September 22, 1902, in a section of New York City called the Lower East Side, which was predomi-

nately inhabited by Jewish people. My parents were Lewis and Esther Levine, and I was the second child of three. My father named me "Bracha," the feminine form of "Baruch," which was his grandfather's Hebrew name and the person whom he worshipped. Baruch amazingly acquired an education in Russia, which was unheard of at that time. His fame was so widespread that the czar employed him. My father told me he named me after him because he felt I, too, would be able to attain any goal I wished. He kept stressing this. I loved and revered my father, though I only knew him for my first five years of life. Upon his death I decided upon two goals, from which I never strayed. One goal was never to be placed in an orphanage, as my younger brother was. This meant that at the point of my father's death and for the rest of her life, I assumed a great deal of responsibility to care for my mother. At age 5, I relieved her of most of the household duties, like housework, preparing meals, doing laundry, etc., so she could remain in good health and would be able to work in a variety of menial jobs. Even after she remarried, when I was 11, I needed to continue this, as her new husband was not a good or reliable breadwinner.

The second big goal was that somewhere in this wonderful land of opportunity I would get an education better than any of my ancestors. I was always an outstanding student, a voracious reader, and took advantage of every opportunity to educate myself. I joined the Henry Street Settlement House, which afforded me wonderful learning opportunities. I graduated from public school at age 11. My stepfather found a job for me in a sewing machine factory, where I worked for a *year and I secreted money from my salary. I then put myself through secretarial school, where I learned shorthand and became very competent, earned a good salary, and always saved. From that I was able to use my savings and put down a deposit on a house for my mother and stepfather in a far section of Brooklyn. Although working full-time, I always went to evening high school in every community my family moved. Finally, after many years, I graduated from high school with honors. Depression years were upon us, but I was determined to get a good education. I was ecstatic to gain acceptance to the University of Michigan, where they had a work/study program so I could pay my tuition, room, and board. I graduated magna cum laude, and my major was sociology. Moving back to New York City, I worked for social services organizations and quickly rose to administrator. I also fell in love and married. All the time my mother lived with me, my husband and our 3 children and I took care of her also. Like my father, my husband died when our children were young. I had to continue working, and I took courses at Columbia University at night. I would not have been able to do this were it not for my mother, who, though arthritic, was responsible for caring for my children so I would not have to hire help I could not afford. My mother's contribution was above and beyond any commitment any mother could make, and I am forever grateful.*

Religion always played a vital role in my life. It started when I learned my father would not have anyone to say Kaddish for him after he died. (Kaddish is the prayer Jews recite when a loved one has died.) I resolved that I would be-

come educated in Yiddish and Hebrew language, particularly reading prayers in Hebrew, which for me was direct communication with God. I say a few of the Hebrew words as an introduction and then talk directly with God. He answers by giving me a feeling of being protected and loved in almost a fatherly fashion, and this has always been very comforting. Because I felt so grounded in Judaism, I decided that in my extensive travels I would study other religions also. I believe that there is one God for all people, though people try to reach Him in different ways. My relationship with God has helped me understand that relationships are the key to all that happens to us in life. When I entered this nursing home, at first I could not accept my loss of independence and my home. I became very depressed and for a brief time wanted to die. However, once I realized that this chapter in my life also has a purpose, I turned my life around. One of those purposes was to thoughtfully review my life and pass on to you, my dear family, the values I have held dear. These values, which I internalized from my father, have grounded and guided me through my life's journey, and I hope they will do the same for you. Also, the relationships I have made here with residents and staff have given me renewed meaning. As I discovered throughout my life, I love people and they love me. We need each other. Daily, staff transmit their great strength, both physical and spiritual, to me with their gentle, healing hands. Their belief in my ability to be all that I can be has deeply inspired me. Judaism, my spiritual fountain, has given me the will to live. I believe I can still do and carry out God's work on Earth in giving to others. God bless all of my friends, and, in the name of my father, I say God bless America, land that I love . . .

I want to leave you, my dear family, with some thoughts. Goals are essential to develop a person's regard for himself and his place both in his home and in the community. One must creatively shape one's life so that it is productive and satisfying. In a country like the United States, there are so many opportunities to develop beyond what your forebearers were able to do because of the educational opportunities available. Education fostered my interest in world affairs, travel, and contact with others that elevated me beyond anything I thought was possible. I traveled widely, even though I had limited resources. I've been to Europe, Africa, South and Central America, Japan. Once in a typhoon in the Sea of Japan, I thought I would lose my life. It made me think about its purpose. You can just plod along, or you can strive to be more. Always remember: the availability of resources is always possible, but the effort has to be yours. Please remember that without family you have neither security nor the spiritual values that give life meaning. I have always felt my family came first—my grandparents, my mother, and my children and grandchildren. Life, no matter what the struggles, the perplexities, always has a value if you value who you are as a human being.

As you see, I have a great need to leave something of myself, as I don't believe I will completely die. The driving spirit that everlastingly pumps joy into this old body at this time will continue forever as my blood courses through you. I hope you will always feel my love and comfort and my em-

brace. Despite all that sadness and difficulties of life that are inevitable, we must always embrace the challenges and keep striving. Don't let life ever defeat you. You have the innate ability to charter your course so that it not only satisfies you but all those you love. I knew my father for a mere 5 years, yet his great desire for me to get a good education and be all that I could be influenced me all my life. My Hebrew name Bracha means "blessing." And I believe that I have been that to honor my father's memory. I want to live in your thoughts lovingly as a guide so you will make more out of your lives than I. In this respect you are keeping my memory alive. Living in memory with love is living forever.

Beatrice Taishoff

July 2001

APPENDIX II
ETHICAL WILL RESOURCES

The following list will provide you with a variety of print, Internet-based, software, and organizational resources that can help you to complete your ethical will.

SELECTED BOOKS AND
PRINT RESOURCES

Albom, Mitch, *Tuesdays With Morrie: An Old Man, A Young Man, and Life's Greatest Lesson*, New York: Doubleday, 1997.

Callanan, Maggie, and Patricia Kelley, *Final Gifts, Understanding the Special Awareness, Needs, and Communications of the Dying*, New York: Bantam Books, 1997.

Covey, Stephen, *The Seven Habits of Highly Effective People*, Simon & Schuster, 1989.

Frankl, Viktor E., *Man's Search for Meaning*, Simon & Schuster, 1959, 1962, 1984.

Freed, Rachael, *Women's Lives, Women's Legacies: Passing on Your Beliefs and Blessings to Future Generations: Creating Your Spiritual-Ethical Will*, Minneapolis, MN: Fairview Press, 2003.

Remen, Rachel Naomi, M.D., *Kitchen Table Wisdom: Stories That Heal*, New York: Riverhead Books, 1996.

Riemer, Jack, and Nathaniel Stampfer, *So That Your Values Live On: Ethical Wills and How to Prepare Them*, Woodstock, VT: Jewish Lights Publishing, 1991.

Schacter-Shalomi, Zalman, and Ronald Miller, *From Ageing to Sage-ing*, New York: Warner Books, 1997.

SOFTWARE RESOURCES

Baines, Barry K., M.D., and Wm. Bradley Rouse, *Putting Your Values on Paper™: The Ethical Will Writing Guide*, 2000. Available via Internet downloading and purchase from www.ethicalwill.com.

INTERNET RESOURCES

www.ethicalwill.com
Operating since 1999, this Web site focuses exclusively on ethical wills. More than thirty ethical will examples are posted on this site. Many links for additional resources are available as well.

ORGANIZATIONAL RESOURCES

The Legacy Center: Dedicated to preserving stories, values, and meaning for individuals, communities, and organizations. 1629 W. 25th St., Minneapolis, MN 55405; Tel: 612-333-2833; e-mail: thelegacycenter@aol.com; Web site: www.thelegacy center.net.

Local community volunteer programs: A number of volunteer programs serving different communities may offer "ethical will coach" volunteers to assist you. These programs may also be interested in offering ethical will mentor training to their volunteers to serve the community.

Appendix III
Living Will Resources

Aging with Dignity is the organization that has produced the popular Five Wishes Advance Directive. This is available for a small fee. This living will is not legal in all states. If you like this form, make sure to check and see that it is legal in your state. Tel: 888-5-WISHES or 850-681-2010; Web site: www.agingwithdignity.org.

Caring Connections, a program of the National Hospice and Palliative Care Organization, provides a variety of free resources on living wills (advance directives) for every state. You can download and print any of these forms. Web site: www.caringinfo.org.

Partnership for Caring is an organization providing current information on advance directive laws in all fifty states. They also have a twenty-four-hour hotline. Free information on advance directives is available. Tel: 800-989-WILL (9455); Web site: www.partnershipforcaring.org.

Books

Caring Conversations Workbook, published by the Midwest Bioethics Center, 1021–1025 Jefferson St., Kansas City, MO 64105. Tel: 816-221-1100; Web site: www.midbio.org.

Norlander, Linda, and Kerstin McSteen. *Choices at the End of Life: Finding Out What Your Parents Want Before It's Too Late.* Minneapolis, MN: Fairview Press, 2001.

APPENDIX IV
EXAMPLES OF
LIVING WILLS

Here are four examples of living wills.

The Living Will of Barry K. Baines

These are my instructions for my health care when I am unable to decide or speak for myself.

The person I choose as my health care agent is

Sandra L. Baines, Address: Tel: Cell:

If Sandra is unavailable or unable to serve as my health care agent, I choose my daughters, Alisha D. Baines, Address: Tel: Cell: and Hannah M. Baines, Address: Tel: Cell: to serve as joint health care agents. Should one be unavailable, the other has the power to act on my behalf.

My health care agent has the authority to make all decisions regarding my health care.

My goals for health care depend on my condition and prognosis.

If I have a condition from which there is little hope of recovery, and I can no longer communicate with others, and I am dependent on others for all of my needs and can no longer participate in activities that bring joy and meaning to my life, then I wish for the following:

I want to be kept comfortable and have all distressing symptoms relieved.

I want to be kept clean.

I want to be cared for at home if at all possible.

I want to have hospice involved in my care if that is appropriate for my prognosis.

I do not want artificial nutrition and hydration or any other treatments that will only prolong my dying and not add to my comfort.

I do not want any other tests that would not add to my comfort.

If there is a reasonable chance of meaningful recovery, I would like a trial of any treatment that would contribute to my recovery. However, this trial should be limited to 3–7 days, after which time, any and all treatments can be discontinued to let nature take its course.

If I can't speak for myself, and my health care agent determines it is in my best interest and the best interest of my family to deviate from these wishes, I give my health care agent the authority to do so.

After death, I want a traditional Jewish funeral (white shroud and the plain pine box).

If Sandra cannot serve as my agent, I request that Alisha and Hannah reach a consensus on all decisions affecting my

health care. In the event they cannot agree between two op-
tions (as a "gambling man") I request that they flip a coin to
decide which decision to make.

This next example was written by a close colleague, Linda
Norlander, who coauthored a book on living wills, titled
Choices at the End of Life: Knowing What Your Parents Want
before It's Too Late.

Linda Norlander's Health Care Directive Instructions

I believe that the health care decisions and measures chosen
for me if I am unable to speak for myself should depend on
the prognosis of my condition and take into consideration the
quality of my life and the quality of my family's life. I want
my health care directive to go into effect and my agent to
make decisions for me under the following circumstances:
    If I am

- *In a condition where my health is progressively deterio-*
  rating due to an eventually fatal illness or condition
- *In a coma with little hope of recovery*
- *In a persistent vegetative state or a persistent state where*
  I have no conscious brain function
- *Suffering from advanced dementia*
- *In a condition where I am dependent on others for all*
  my physical needs and cannot communicate (such as ad-
  vanced ALS)

I want

- *Comfort care only*
- *My pain and other physical symptoms managed*
- *Hospice care at home if possible*
- *Short-term life support such as a respirator for the purposes of organ donation only*

I do not want

- *Feeding tubes or artificial nutrition and hydration that will only prolong my dying and not add to my comfort or quality of life*
- *Tests or procedures that will not add to my comfort*
- *Resuscitation or intubation (except for purposes of organ donation)*
- *My care to place an extreme financial or care giving burden on my family*
- *Politicians and extremist religious groups involved in my health care decisions*

These are my wishes based on my best attempt to imagine future circumstances. However, if I am unable to make and communicate my own decisions and my health care agent decides it is in the best interest of my family and myself to deviate from what is stated here, I give him full and final authority to do so.

A close friend and colleague, Rachael Freed, a clinical social worker and author of *Women's Lives, Women's Legacies:*

Passing Your Beliefs and Blessings to Future Generations (Creating Your Own Spiritual-Ethical Will), wrote the following example. I've included an excerpt of a letter that Rachael wrote to her children to accompany her living will. She hoped that the letter would open and ease family conversation about her end-of-life wishes.

Minnesota Health Care Directive
of Rachael A. Freed

My personal information: Rachael A. Freed: Address, Home Telephone, Cell Phone

Health care agent(s):

I appoint two people, my son, Sidney Loren Levin, and/ or my daughter, Deborah Levin Stillman, to serve as my primary-joint health care agents, or should one be unavailable, the other has the power to act on my behalf. And as alternate agent, I appoint Sandra Swirnoff, who I suggest my son and daughter include to assist them in coming to agreement when making decisions for me.

Sidney Loren Levin: Address and Telephone Contact Numbers

Deborah Levin Stillman: Address and Telephone Contact Numbers

Sandra Swirnoff: Address and Telephone Contact Numbers

Powers of my agent(s):

If I am unable to decide or speak for myself, my agent(s) have the power to

- *Interpret all instructions I have given in this form, attached additional instructions, or in discussion, according to their understanding of my wishes and values*
- *See and approve release of my medical records and personal files for health purposes. Obtain copies of my medical records and allow others to see them. If my signature is required to get any of these records, my agent(s) can sign for me*
- *Apply for Medicare, Medicaid, or other programs or insurance benefits for me; see my personal files, including all financial records, to get the information needed to fill out any forms*
- *Take any legal action needed to carry out my wishes*
- *Make choices for me about my medical care or services, including tests, medicine, procedures, and surgery*
- *Consent to, refuse, or withdraw any health care, treatment, service, or procedure, including artificially provided food and water, to keep me alive*
- *Choose my health care providers, hire (and fire if needed) any kind of health care worker I may need to help me or take care of me*
- *Choose where I live when I need health care and what personal security measures are needed to keep me safe; arrange for admission to a hospital, hospice, or nursing home for me; move me to another state to carry out my wishes or for other reasons*

I also authorize my agent(s) to

- *Carry out my wishes regarding what will happen to my body when I die, a memorial service, and burial*
- *Make decisions about mental health treatment including antipsychotic medication but excluding electroconvulsive therapy*

Health care instructions:

I, Rachael A. Freed, born November 8, 1938, being an adult of sound mind, have prepared this document as a directive to be followed for my end-of-life care. I understand that my health care providers are legally bound to act consistent with my wishes, within the limits of reasonable medical practice and applicable law. My agents are empowered to act in accordance with my wishes and values if I am unable to participate in decisions regarding my health care because of injury, accident, or illness.

When the quality of my life has diminished due to accident, injury, or illness and the prognosis that the injury or illness is irreversible and "terminal," I direct my health care agents, my family, my physician, my lawyer, my health care providers, and all other persons whom it may concern to do no act or procedure that would principally serve to prolong the dying process or attempt to avoid death. However, I do want to be treated with dignity, love, and respect for my wishes and values as I approach death. To that end, I detail the following instructions regarding aspects of my care:

Life-prolonging treatment: If the prognosis of an accident, injury, or illness suggests a reasonable chance of both physical and mental recovery, I want every life-prolonging treatment to be utilized. I define a "reasonable recovery" as being able to enjoy everyday life, socially relate to my loved ones, and be of some service to others.

If, on the other hand, I have severe dementia or confusion and my condition will only worsen, or if I have a severe and permanent brain injury and there is little or no chance of regaining consciousness, or if I have a terminal illness that cannot be reversed by any known or experimental treatment, I do not want my life prolonged by any medications, artificial means, or other mechanical treatments, including but not limited to (a) treatment with antibiotics if pneumonia or other infection develops; (b) electrical or mechanical resuscitation of my heart; (c) feeding tube in nose, stomach, intestine, or veins when I am no longer able to swallow; (d) mechanical respiration when my brain can no longer sustain my own breathing; and (e) renal dialysis, amputations, surgery, or any other procedure.

If any of the above are necessary to temporarily prolong my life exclusively to make tissue, body parts, or organs of mine available for research or transplant to other persons, I would wish it.

If feeding of liquids or solids by intravenous measures would provide me comfort and freedom of pain, even if they would prolong life, I would wish it.

Pain control: I wish to be given medication to control pain, to make me as comfortable and as free from pain as possible, even if it shortens my life. Assuming that my ability to think and communicate is not diminished, I want pain medications that will allow me to be as conscious and aware as possible.

Comfort preferences: *I wish to be kept fresh and clean; I wish to have my clothes and bed linen kept clean and changed if I have soiled them; I wish to have personal care (nails, teeth, and hair); I want such things as a cool cloth on my head if I have a fever, my lips and mouth kept moist if I am no longer taking food or fluids. I wish for green plants and fresh flowers, perhaps a rock or two where I can see them, along with pictures of my children and grandchildren (and great grandchildren).*

Spiritual and social preferences: I wish to be visited by my rabbis and have end-of-life rituals of our Reform Jewish tradition be practiced. I wish to be named on the healing prayer list at services. I wish to have family and friends visit, talk with me, read to me, share memories and stories, touch me, hold my hand, kiss me, pray for me. I wish to be cared for with kindness and dignity. I want to die at home, if possible, and I want someone to be with me when death is imminent. I want my family's experience of my dying to be of intimacy, honesty, a meaningful and natural part of the cycle of life that we share.

X Yes, I have attached a letter of additional instructions and explanation of my preferences and values concerning my end of life care.

X Yes, I authorize donation of organs, tissue, and/or other body parts after my death.

X The following page makes this document legal. I and witnesses have signed and dated it. I will distribute copies to my agents, family members, physician, attorney, and other health care personnel.

Letter to Accompany My Minnesota
Advance Health Care Directive

To my children, Sid and Debbie,

This letter, accompanying my Minnesota Advance Health Care Directive, is to tell you in narrative form what I hope for in relation to my dying and death. At sixty-six, having lived beyond my own mother by nine years, it seems an appropriate time to write this. Although I consider myself in very good health, although somewhat overweight, I am vital and interested in the varied and stimulating aspects of my life. I hope to live a long time and consider myself a good candidate to be one of those centurions (is that someone who lives to be 100, or am I volunteering to be a soldier in the Roman Army?).

My intention is to review this letter and other documents annually, as situations change rapidly.

Although the accompanying legal document (2 pages + legal notary) spells out care decisions, medical treatment, etc., my purpose here is to write you about the things I have concerns about, to explain them so that you will have no questions about my desires, perspective, and values. I hope that you will not only allow me to have my way but that you will support and advocate for me when and if the time comes that I need your love to be expressed by that advocacy. In Genesis 47:29 (I am neither being arcane nor erudite . . . this happens to be the parashah of the ethical will of Jacob), Jacob asks Joseph to pledge his loyalty by agreeing to bury him with his ancestors. Midrashic commentary defines this hesed v'emet

184

as true kindness, explicating that such a deed is one for which no reciprocal favor can be anticipated.

I have asked both of you, Sid and/or Deb, not only for this hesed v'emet, but to jointly be "my agents." I don't want this to cause dissension between the two of you. I believe that you will be able to agree on decisions that need to be made. I hope that the two of you will have an easier time dealing with my dying and death because you will be together and can support each other in what can be a difficult time. That's the "and" in jointly, but I am also establishing the agentship as "or" so that if one of you is unavailable, the other will have the power to act on my behalf.

With her permission, I have asked Sandy Swirnoff to be the "alternate agent," and if she is available, I would like for you to include her in your discussions and decisions about my end-of-life care. We have had many conversations about dying, and she will be of help to you and to me as someone who knows about death and dying, has had experience close up with some of the difficulties between health care providers and family members, and can function as a tiebreaker mediator, should there be a decision that the two of you cannot agree on.

I believe the only hard decision could be when . . . when is the turning point when there is no longer hope of recovery or a reasonable quality of life possible? For your edification, quality of life for me is not about my body but life from the neck up (as I have lived most of my life up to now); it includes my feelings and my thoughts, my emotional, mental, and spiritual life. If I were to be physically immobilized, I still could experience the joy of love and learning. But should I not be able to feel, think, and communicate in some way, then for me that is not life.

On the other hand, at this moment when I am just 66, I believe the decision may not be simple or clear and that circumstances and age are factors for you to take into account. A friend (age 55) in England had respiratory distress with flu, was put on life support, and at first got progressively worse. Her family was informed that she would likely not survive. After three full weeks on life support, she has survived, is out of the hospital, at home, and being told that she should have full recovery. So please look at both sides, and don't pull the plug too quickly or be too sure that miracles don't happen!

Once you have agreed that the turning point has come, that the when is now, then the decisions are about the kind of medical treatment I want and don't want, my comfort, how I want people, including professional caregivers, to treat me, and how I want to be memorialized.

I want to be comfortable and pain-free and not have my life prolonged by any medical interventions that are life-prolonging, except for those that would allow me to die comfortably (a taste of couscous, a glass of Pinot Grigio to moisten my lips . . . you get the idea). I hope that when the time comes, there will be medications to alleviate pain but that allow me to be conscious and aware and as responsive as I choose to be until the end.

If my dying involves dementia and/or Alzheimer's and of my not being the "me" that we all, including me, know and love, I want to be made comfortable, visited as often as you

186

*can emotionally manage, and allowed to die naturally (pneu-
monia, etc.) with no resuscitation, invasive procedures, or
medications to prolong my life. Since all the financial arrangements are in place and you already have control over my financial estate, I don't assume that any mental loss on my part
would put the legal-financial aspect of my life in jeopardy.*

*Of course, I hope that I'll just not wake up one morning,
and you will not have to make difficult decisions, but that's not
how most people die. Although I have much to live for, lots of
love to give and receive, and continuing curiosity, delight in
learning and travel, in teaching and inspiring others, and
want to play more than I did in the first 60 years of my life, if
I did die tomorrow, I have had a blessed, full, and satisfying
life. My only regret would be not being present (although
maybe I will be in some way; I don't have any way of knowing
while yet alive) to cheer on your lives and my grandchildren's.*

*. . . This was far less difficult to write than I'd imagined. It
actually gives me a sense of relief, of peace, to both acknowledge my own mortality and the blessing it is to live in a time
when one can speak about it and in a time when there is hope
for a pain-free conscious death, and the best blessing of all, to
have you two children whom I love more than my life and
who love me enough to take care of my end-of-life needs.*

Thank you, Mom

This last example is unique in that it combines the elements of an ethical will into a living will. The author of this
document is a nurse by profession and the mother of three
children. Joan was in her late fifties when she wrote this.

In the event that I cannot make my own health care deci-sions, there are no other people I trust more to make these decisions than the three of you. The three of you are growing into people I am proud to call my children and my friends. Each of you has different strengths, and together you are a great team.

I am writing down a few of my wishes and values to guide you in the decisions, if you have to make them. Being inde-pendent is a value that I hold very near and dear to my heart.

I remember as a small child hearing a consistent challenge from my father: one should always be prepared to care for themselves and be their own person. So much of what I am is because of Grandpa, and I dearly miss him every day. Each of you was lucky to have him in your life. And looking at how independent each child in his family has turned out, I think he is smiling at us each day (probably from a boat when he is out fishing).

If I am in a life-threatening situation where the outcome is most probably going to be a state of dependency, I do not want any extraordinary means employed to keep me alive. I do not want to be maintained on a respirator, receive artifi-cial feedings, or have people resuscitate me if my heart stops. Death is not really the enemy, and I believe in another life af-ter death. Death does not scare me, but living without any quality does. I like being a part of each of your lives and hav-ing a life of my own. Just being maintained with bodily sys-tems is not my definition of living.

If I am paralyzed and cannot breathe on my own, if I have a critical head injury, if I suffer a large burn, if I have a sig-

nificant neurological event or require surgery that is only palliative, I want you to consider the outcome. What would be important to me is to be kept comfortable, free of pain, and have my family close by during my dying process.

These examples do not address every situation; they are just examples. Use your judgment. I trust you to make good choices.

If I am to die and can help another by donating organs, that is a practice I am in favor of. I would live on in each of you but just maybe in someone else also. However, if any one of the three of you is opposed to this and does not feel comfortable, do not feel obligated to agree to donation. I have found this is a very private decision and makes some people uncomfortable.

I want my children to speak for my health care needs if I cannot. Please support them in these decisions, which they will make based on my values. I have seen people question decisions, especially if they are not the decisions they would like made. Please don't do this. Health care decisions are hard to make, and people do not need to be second-guessed.

I have a great life. I have three children I am proud of, an extended family that will be there for support, and a circle of friends that I cannot even begin to explain their importance. I have had fun, and I see my life as an adventure. Humor ought to be a large part of every person's day. Every day there is a new mountain to climb. Some adventures are not much fun and do not turn out the way you want them to, but all of them shape who you are. I always make myself try to do new things because I swore never to get complacent and do only what is comfortable. This year I have made a decision that changed the makeup of our family, truly the most difficult decision I have ever made. Time will tell whether it is the right decision.

In the future, I challenge the three of you to always be willing to climb new mountains and greet new adventures. I want to see a future where each of you is happy, that you make supportive and provocative mates if you marry, attentive parents who challenge any children that come, supportive family to your extended family, and a loyal friend to those you choose to call friends. Karen Kaiser Clark talks of growing deep, not just tall. I heard her speak years ago, but I have never forgotten that statement.

The other concept that has guided me was in a book by Viktor Frankl. The concept emphasized what we can control in our lives. We cannot control so much that happens to or around us, but we can control how we choose to react to what happens to us. I cannot tell you how much this concept has helped me. It gives me a sense of control in situations even when I cannot control any of the events. And it helps me put events in perspective.

As I close here, I have to chuckle because I realize, even at the end of my life, I do not stop giving directions. Humor me, it is who I am.

Love, Mom

APPENDIX V
SAMPLE HEALTHCARE
DIRECTIVE FORMS

191

Healthcare Treatment Directive

I, _____ , SS#_____ want everyone who cares for me to know what healthcare I want.
(Optional)
I always expect to be given care and treatment for pain or discomfort even if such care may affect how I sleep, eat, or breathe.

I want my dying to be as natural as possible. Therefore, I direct that no treatment (including food or water by tube) be given just to keep my body functioning when I have
• a condition that will cause me to die soon, or
• a condition so bad (including substantial brain damage or brain disease) that I have no reasonable hope of achieving a quality of life that is acceptable to me.

An acceptable quality of life to me is one that includes the following capacities and values. (Describe here the things that are most important to you when you are making decisions to choose or refuse life-sustaining treatments.)
_____
_____
_____
_____

Examples:	• recognize family or friends	• make decisions	• communicate
	• feed myself	• take care of myself	• be responsive to my environment

I want my doctor to try treatments on a time-limited basis when the goal is to restore my health or help me experience a life in a way consistent with my values and wishes. I want such treatments withdrawn when they cannot achieve this goal or become too burdensome to me.

Among the time-limited treatments I would not agree to under any circumstances are the following: _____
_____

Examples:	• resuscitation (CPR)	• dialysis	• ventilator
	• food or water by tube	• chemotherapy	• transfusions
	• antibiotics	• surgery	

☐ In facing the end of my life, I expect my agent (if I have one) and my caregivers to honor my wishes, values, and directives.
☐ For further clarification, please refer to my Caring Conversations Workbook, which is located at _____ .

**Be Sure to sign the reverse side of this page even if you do not wish
to appoint a Durable Power of Attorney for Healthcare Decisions**

If you only want to name a Durable Power of Attorney for Healthcare Decisions, draw a large X through this page.

Talk about this form and your ideas about your healthcare with the person you have chosen to make decisions for you, your doctors, family, friends, and clergy. Give each of them a completed copy.

You may cancel or change this form at any time. You should review it often. Each time you review it, put your initials and the date here. _____

This document is provided as a service by the Center for Practical Bioethics.
For more information, call the Center for Practical Bioethics 816-221-1100
E-mail – bioethic@practicalbioethics.org • Web site – www.practicalbioethics.org

Durable Power of Attorney for Healthcare Decisions
■ *Take a copy of this with you whenever you go to the hospital or on a trip* ■

It is important to choose someone to make healthcare decisions for you when you cannot make or communicate decisions for yourself. Tell the person you choose what healthcare treatments you want. The person you choose will be your agent. He or she will have the right to make decisions for your healthcare. If you DO NOT choose someone to make decisions for you, write NONE on the line for the agent's name.

I, _____, SS#_____, appoint the person named in this document to be my agent to make my healthcare decisions.
        (optional)

This document is a Durable Power of Attorney for Healthcare Decisions. My agent's power shall not end if I become incapacitated or if there is uncertainty that I am dead. This document revokes any prior Durable Power of Attorney for Healthcare Decisions. My agent may not appoint anyone else to make decisions for me. My agent and caregivers are protected from any claims based on following this Durable Power of Attorney for Healthcare. My agent shall not be responsible for any costs associated with my care. I give my agent full power to make all decisions for me about my healthcare, including the power to direct the withholding or withdrawal of life-prolonging treatment, including artificially supplied nutrition and hydration/tube feeding. My agent is authorized to

- Consent, refuse, or withdraw consent to any care, procedure, treatment, or service to diagnose, treat, or maintain a physical or mental condition;
- Make all necessary arrangements for any hospital, psychiatric treatment facility, hospice, nursing home, or other healthcare organization; and, employ or discharge healthcare personnel (any person who is authorized or permitted by the laws of the state to provide healthcare services) as he or she shall deem necessary for my physical, mental, or emotional well-being;
- Request, receive, review, and authorize sending any information regarding my physical or mental health, or my personal affairs, including medical and hospital records; and execute any releases that may be required to obtain such information;
- Move me into or out of any State or institution;
- Take legal action, if needed;
- Make decisions about autopsy and tissue and organ donation, and the disposition of my body in conformity with state law; and
- Become my guardian if one is needed.

In exercising this power, I expect my agent to be guided by my directions as we discussed them prior to this appointment and/or to be guided by my Healthcare Directive *(see reverse side)*.

If you DO NOT want the person (agent) you name to be able to do one or other of the above things, draw a line through the statement and put your initials at the end of the line.

Agent's name _____ Phone _____ Email_____
Address_____

*If you do **not** want to name an alternate, write "none."*

First Alternate Agent_____   Second Alternate Agent_____
Name _____   Name_____
Address _____   Address_____
Phone _____   Phone_____
Email _____   Email_____

Effective Date of Appointment (initial the option that best reflects your wishes)

My agent's authority shall take effect immediately upon my signing of this document. _____
My agent's authority shall be effective when and only when I cannot make healthcare decisions for myself. _____

(Be sure that you initialed one, and only one, of the above two options.)

SIGN HERE for the *Durable Power of Attorney* and/or *Health Care Directive* forms. Many states require notarization. It is recommended for the residents of all states. Please ask two persons to witness your signature who are not related to you or financially connected to your estate.

Signature _____ Date _____
Witness _____ Date _____ Witness _____ Date _____

Notarization:
On this _____ day of _____, in the year of _____, personally appeared before me the person signing, known by me to be the person who completed this document and acknowledged it as his/her free act and deed. IN WITNESS WHEREOF, I have set my hand and affixed my official seal in the County of _____, State of _____, on the date written above.

Notary Public_____ Commission Expires _____

APPENDIX V

MINNESOTA
Advance Directive
Planning for Important Healthcare Decisions

Caring Connections, 1700 Diagonal Road, Suite 625, Alexandria, VA 22314
www.caringinfo.org, 800/658-8898

Caring Connections, a program of the National Hospice and Palliative Care Organization (NHPCO), is a national consumer engagement initiative to improve care at the end of life, supported by a grant from The Robert Wood Johnson Foundation.

The goal of Caring Connections is for consumers to hear a unified message promoting awareness and action for improved end-of-life care. Through these efforts, NHPCO seeks to support those working across the country to improve end-of-life care and conditions for all Americans.

Caring Connections tracks and monitors all state and federal legislation and significant court cases related to end-of-life care to ensure that our advance directives are always up to date.

CARING CONNECTIONS

HelpLine

You can call our toll-free HelpLine, 800/658-8898, if you have any difficulty understanding your state-specific advance directive, or if you are dealing with a difficult end-of-life situation and need immediate information. We can help provide resources and information on questions like these:

- How do I communicate my end-of-life wishes to my family?
- What type of end-of-life care is available to me?
- What questions should I ask my mother's doctors about her end-of-life care?

It's About How You LIVE

It's About How You LIVE is a national community engagement campaign encouraging individuals to make informed decisions about end-of-life care and services. The campaign encourages people to:

Learn about options for end-of-life services and care
Implement plans to ensure wishes are honored
Voice decisions to family, friends and health care providers
Engage in personal or community efforts to improve end-of-life care

Please call the HelpLine at 800/658-8898 to learn more about the LIVE campaign, obtain free resources, or to join the effort to improve community, state and national end-of-life care.

APPENDIX V

HOW TO USE THESE MATERIALS

1. Check to be sure that you have the materials for your state. You should complete a form for the state in which you expect to receive health care.

2. These materials include:
   - Instructions for preparing your advance directive.
   - Your state-specific advance directive forms, which are the pages with the gray instruction bar on the left side.

3. Read the instructions in their entirety. They give you specific information about the requirements in your state.

4. You may want to photocopy these forms before you start so you will have a clean copy if you need to start over.

5. When you begin to complete the form, refer to the gray instruction bars - they indicate where you need to mark, insert your personal instructions, or sign the form.

6. Talk with your family, friends, and physicians about your decision to complete an advance directive. Be sure the person you appoint to make decision on your behalf understands your wishes.

If you have questions or need guidance in preparing your advance directive or about what you should do with it after you have completed it, you may call our toll free number 800/ 658-8898 and a staff member will be glad to assist you.

For more information contact:

**The National Hospice and Palliative Care Organization
1700 Diagonal Road, Suite 625
Alexandria, VA 22314**

**Call our HelpLine: 800/658-8898
Visit our Web site: www.caringinfo.org**

Formerly a publication of Last Acts Partnership.

Support for this program is provided by a grant from
The Robert Wood Johnson Foundation, Princeton,
New Jersey.

INTRODUCTION TO YOUR MINNESOTA HEALTH-CARE DIRECTIVE

This packet contains a legal document, the Minnesota Health-Care Directive, that protects your right to refuse medical treatment you do not want, or to request treatment you do want, in the event you lose the ability to make decisions yourself.

1. Part I, **Appointment of Health Care Agent**, lets you name someone to make decisions about your medical care—including decisions about life support—if you can no longer speak for yourself or immediately if you specify this in the document. The Appointment of Health Care Agent is especially useful because it appoints someone to speak for you any time you cannot make your own medical decisions, not only at the end of life.

2. Part II, **Health Care Instructions**, functions as your state's living will. It lets you state your wishes about medical care in the event that you can no longer make your own medical decisions.

Although you have the option to complete only one part of this document, Caring Connections suggests that you complete Part I and Part II to best ensure that you receive the medical care you want when you can no longer speak for yourself.

Note: These documents will be legally binding only if the person completing them is a competent adult who is 18 years of age or older.

How do I make my Health-Care Directive legal?
In order to make your Health-Care Directive legally binding you have two options:

1. Sign your document in the presence of two witnesses, who must also sign the document. Both of your witnesses cannot:
   - be under the age of 18,
   - be the person you appointed as your agent or alternate agent,

In addition, one of your witnesses cannot be:
   - your health care provider, or an employee of your health-care provider.

OR

2. Sign your document in the presence of a notary public. The person notarizing your health care directive may be an employee of a health care provider providing you with direct care.

COMPLETING PART I: APPOINTMENT OF HEALTH CARE AGENT

Whom should I appoint as my agent?

A health care agent is the person you appoint to make decisions about your medical care if you become unable to make these decisions yourself. Your agent can be a family member or a close friend whom you trust to make serious decisions. The person you name as your agent should clearly understand your wishes and be willing to accept the responsibility of making medical decisions for you.

You **cannot** appoint the following persons as your agent unless they are related to you by blood, marriage, registered domestic partnership, or adoption:

- your health care provider on the date you sign your health care directive or on the date your health care agent must make decisions for you;
- an employee of your health care provider on the date you sign your health care directive or on the date your health care agent must make decisions for you.

You can appoint a second person as your alternative agent. An alternative agent will step in if the person you name as agent is unable, unwilling or unavailable to act for you.

Should I add personal instructions to my Appointment of Health Care Agent?

You can use the space provided to limit your agent's authority. Caring Connections recommends that you not place restrictions on your agent. One of the strongest reasons for naming a health care agent is to have someone who can respond flexibly as your medical condition changes and can deal with situations that you did not foresee. Unless the form you sign limits the authority of your agent, your agent may make all health care decisions for you including:

- the power to give, refuse, or withdraw consent to any care, treatment, service, or procedures. This includes deciding whether to stop or not start health care that is keeping you or might keep you alive, and deciding about intrusive mental health treatment;
- choosing your health care providers;
- deciding where you live and receive care and support when those choices relate to your health care needs;
- the right to review your medical records and have the same rights that you would have to give your records to other people.

We urge you to talk with your health care agent about your future medical care and describe what you consider to be an acceptable "quality of life". If you want to record your wishes about specific treatments or conditions, you can use Part II of this document, Health Care Instructions.

COMPLETING PART II: HEALTH CARE INSTRUCTIONS

Are there personal instructions I should add to my Health Care Instructions?

If you have appointed an agent, it is a good idea to write a statement such as, "Any questions about how to interpret or when to apply my Health Care Instructions are to be decided by my agent."

If you are a woman of childbearing age and would like your Minnesota Health Care Instructions to be honored even if you are pregnant, then you must state this in the Health Care Instructions.

It is important to learn about the kinds of life-sustaining treatment you might receive. Consult your doctor or order the Caring Connections booklet, "Advance Directives and End-of-Life Decisions."

IMPORTANT FACTS

You may revoke your Health Care Directive using any one of the following methods:

- sign a new directive;
- cancel, deface, obliterate, burn, tear or otherwise destroy your Directive;
- sign a written and dated statement indicating that you wish to revoke your Directive, in whole or in part, or;
- verbally express your intent to revoke your Directive, in whole or in part, in the presence of two witnesses who do not have to be present at the same time.

AFTER YOU HAVE COMPLETED YOUR DOCUMENTS

1. Your Minnesota Health-Care Directive is an important legal document. Keep the original signed document in a secure but accessible place. Do not put the original document in a safe deposit box or any other security box that would keep others from having access to it.

2. Give photocopies of the signed original to your agent and alternate agent(s), doctor(s), family, close friends, clergy and anyone else who might become involved in your health care. If you enter a nursing home or hospital, have photocopies of your document placed in your medical records.

3. Be sure to talk to your agent and alternate agent(s), doctor(s), clergy, family and friends about your wishes concerning medical treatment. Discuss your wishes with them often, particularly if your medical condition changes.

4. If you want to make changes to your document after it has been signed and witnessed, you should complete a new document.

5. Remember, you can always revoke one or both sections of your Minnesota Health-Care Directive.

6. Be aware that your Minnesota documents will not be effective in the event of a medical emergency. Ambulance personnel are required to provide cardiopulmonary resuscitation (CPR) unless they are given a separate order that states otherwise. These orders, commonly called "non-hospital do-not-resuscitate orders," are designed for people whose poor health gives them little chance of benefiting from CPR. These orders must be signed by your physician and instruct ambulance personnel not to attempt CPR if your heart or breathing should stop. Currently not all states have laws authorizing non-hospital do-not-resuscitate orders. Caring Connections does not distribute these forms. We suggest you speak to your physician.

If you would like more information about this topic contact Caring Connections or consult the Caring Connections booklet "Cardiopulmonary Resuscitation, Do-Not-Resuscitate Orders and End-Of-Life Decisions."

APPENDIX V

MINNESOTA HEALTH CARE DIRECTIVE – PAGE 1 OF 8

I, _____, understand this document allows me to do ONE or BOTH of the following:

PART I: Name another person (called the health care agent) to make health care decisions for me if I am unable to decide or speak for myself. My health care agent must make health care decisions for me based on the instructions I provide in this document (Part II), if any, the wishes I have made known to him or her, or must act in my best interest if I have not made my health care wishes known.

AND/OR

Part II: Give health care instructions to guide others making health care decisions for me. If I have named a health care agent, these instructions are to be used by the agent. These instructions may also be used by my health care providers, others assisting with my health care and my family, in the event I cannot make decisions for myself.

PART I: APPOINTMENT OF HEALTH CARE AGENT
THIS IS WHO I WANT TO MAKE HEALTH CARE DECISIONS FOR ME IF I AM UNABLE TO DECIDE OR SPEAK FOR MYSELF

(I know I can change my agent or alternate agent at any time and I know I do not have to appoint an agent or an alternate agent.)

Note: If you appoint an agent, you should discuss this health care directive with your agent and give your agent a copy. If you do not wish to appoint an agent, you may leave Part I blank and go to Part II.

When I am unable to decide or speak for myself, I trust and appoint

_____ to make health care decisions for me. This person is called my health care agent.

Relationship of my health care agent to me: _____

Telephone number of my health care agent: _____

Address of my health care agent:

_____

- -

MINNESOTA HEALTH CARE DIRECTIVE - PAGE 2 OF 8

(OPTIONAL)
APPOINTMENT OF ALTERNATE HEALTH CARE AGENT:

If my health care agent is not reasonably available, I trust and appoint

_____ to be my health care

agent instead.

Relationship of my alternate health care agent to me: _____

Telephone number of my alternate health care agent: _____

Address of my alternate health care agent:

_____

_____

THIS IS WHAT I WANT MY HEALTH CARE AGENT TO BE ABLE
TO DO IF I AM UNABLE TO DECIDE OR SPEAK FOR MYSELF
(I know I can change these choices)

My health care agent is automatically given the powers listed below in (A) through (D). My health care agent must follow my health care instructions in this document or any other instructions I have given to my agent. If I have not given health care instructions, then my agent must act in my best interest.

Whenever I am unable to decide or speak for myself, my health care agent has the power to:
(A) Make any health care decision for me. This includes the power to give, refuse, or withdraw consent to any care, treatment, service, or procedures. This includes deciding whether to stop or not start health care that is keeping me or might keep me alive, and deciding about intrusive mental health treatment.
(B) Choose my health care providers.
(C) Choose where I live and receive care and support when those choices relate to my health care needs.
(D) Review my medical records and have the same rights that I would have to give my medical records to other people.

If I DO NOT want my health care agent to have a power listed above in (A) through (D) OR if I want to LIMIT any power in (A) through (D), I MUST say that here:

PRINT THE NAME, RELATIONSHIP, ADDRESS AND TELEPHONE NUMBER OF YOUR ALTERNATE AGENT

ADD PERSONAL INSTRUCTIONS (ONLY IF YOU WANT TO LIMIT THE POWER OF YOUR AGENT)

MINNESOTA HEALTH CARE DIRECTIVE - PAGE 3 OF 8

My health care agent is NOT automatically given the powers listed below in (1) and (2). If I WANT my agent to have any of the powers in (1) and (2), I must INITIAL the line in front of the power; then my agent WILL HAVE that power.

_____ (1) To decide whether to donate any parts of my body, including organs, tissues, and eyes, when I die.

_____ (2) To decide what will happen with my body when I die (burial, cremation).

If I want to say anything more about my health care agent's powers or limits on the powers, I can say it here:

PART II: HEALTH CARE INSTRUCTIONS

Note: Complete this Part II if you wish to give health care instructions. If you appointed an agent in Part I, completing this Part II is optional but would be very helpful to your agent. However, if you chose not to appoint an agent in Part I, you MUST complete some or all of this Part II if you wish to make a valid health care directive.

These are instructions for my health care when I am unable to decide or speak for myself. These instructions must be followed (so long as they address my needs).

THESE ARE MY BELIEFS AND VALUES ABOUT MY HEALTH CARE
(I know I can change these choices or leave any of them blank.)

I want you to know these things about me to help you make decisions about my health care:

My goals for my health care:

My fears about my health care:

My spiritual or religious beliefs and traditions:

My beliefs about when life would be no longer worth living:

My thoughts about how my medical condition might affect my family:

THIS IS WHAT I WANT AND DO NOT WANT FOR MY HEALTH CARE
(I know I can change these choices or leave any of them blank.)

Many medical treatments may be used to try to improve my medical condition or to prolong my life. Examples include artificial breathing by a machine connected to a tube in the lungs, artificial feeding or fluids through tubes, attempts to start a stopped heart, surgeries, dialysis, antibiotics, and blood transfusions. Most medical treatments can be tried for a while and then stopped if they do not help. I have these views about my health care in these situations:

(Note: You can discuss general feelings, specific treatments, or leave any of them blank.)

If I had a reasonable chance of recovery, and were temporarily unable to decide or speak for myself, I would want:

If I were dying and unable to decide or speak for myself, I would want:

If I were permanently unconscious and unable to decide or speak for myself, I would want:

If I were completely dependent on others for my care and unable to decide or speak for myself, I would want:

In all circumstances, my doctors will try to keep me comfortable and reduce my pain. This is how I feel about pain relief if it would affect my alertness or if it could shorten my life:

There are other things that I want or do not want for my health care, if possible:
Who I would like to be my doctor:

Where I would like to live to receive health care:

Where I would like to die and other wishes I have about dying:

My wishes about donating parts of my body when I die:

My wishes about what happens to my body when I die (cremation, burial):

204

APPENDIX V

ADD OTHER PERSONAL INSTRUCTIONS (IF ANY)

Any other things:

PART III: MAKING THE DOCUMENT LEGAL

This document must be signed by me. It also must either be verified by a notary public (Option 1) OR witnessed by two witnesses (option 2). It must be dated when it is verified or witnessed.

I am thinking clearly, I agree with everything that is written in this document, and I have made this document willingly.

SIGN AND DATE THE DOCUMENT PRINT YOUR DATE OF BIRTH AND ADDRESS

_____

My Signature

Date signed: _____

Date of birth: _____

Address: _____

ONLY COMPLETE THIS SECTION IF YOU WERE UNABLE TO SIGN & SOMEONE ELSE SIGNED FOR YOU

If I cannot sign my name, I can ask someone to sign this document for me.

_____
Signature of the person who I asked to sign this document for me.

_____
Printed name of the person who I asked to sign this document for me.

205

APPENDIX V

OPTION 1: NOTARY PUBLIC

In my presence on _____ (date),

_____ (name) acknowledged his/her signature on this document or acknowledged that he/she authorized the person signing this document to sign on his/her behalf. I am not named as a health care agent or alternate health care agent in this document.

_____
(Signature of Notary)   (Notary Stamp)

OPTION 2: TWO WITNESSES

Two witnesses must sign. Only one of the two witnesses can be a health care provider or an employee of a health care provider giving direct care to me on the day I sign this document.

WITNESS ONE:

(i) In my presence on _____ (date),

_____ (name) acknowledged his/her signature on this document or acknowledged that he/she authorized the person signing this document to sign on his/her behalf.

(ii) I am at least 18 years of age.
(iii) I am not named as a health care agent or an alternate health care agent in this document.
(iv) If I am a health care provider or an employee of a health care provider giving direct care to the person listed above in (A), I must initial this box: [   ]

I certify that the information in (i) through (iv) is true and correct.

_____   _____
(Signature of Witness One)   (Date)

Address: _____

_ _

MINNESOTA HEALTH CARE DIRECTIVE - PAGE 8 OF 8

WITNESS TWO:

(i) In my presence on _____ (date),

_____ (name) acknowledged
his/her signature on this document or acknowledged that he/she authorized the
person signing this document to sign on his/her behalf.

(ii) I am at least 18 years of age.
(iii) I am not named as a health care agent or an alternate health care agent in this
document.
(iv) If I am a health care provider or an employee of a health care provider giving
direct care to the person listed above in (A), I must initial this box: [ ]

I certify that the information in (i) through (iv) is true and correct.

_____   _____
(Signature of Witness Two)   (Date)

Address: _____

- -

Reminder: Keep this document with your personal papers in a safe place (not in a
safe deposit box). Give photocopies of the signed original to your doctors, family,
close friends, health care agent, and alternate health care agent. Make sure you
doctor is willing to follow your wishes. This document should be part of your
medical record at your physician's office and at the hospital, home care agency,
hospice, or nursing facility where you receive your care.

*Courtesy of Caring Connections
1700 Diagonal Road, Suite 625, Alexandria, VA 22314
www.caringinfo.org, 800/658-8898*

NOTES

INTRODUCTION

The statistic regarding how many Americans have a living will was taken from Angela Fagerlin and Carl E. Schneider, "Enough: The Failure of the Living Will," *Hastings Center Report* 34, no. 2 (2004): 30–42.

CHAPTER ONE

I first heard about the tradition of ethical wills in the late 1980s. I recall reading an earlier version of Jack Riemer and Nathaniel Stampfer's *So That Your Values Live On: Ethical Wills and How to Prepare Them* (Woodstock, VT: Jewish Lights, 1991). I read more about ethical wills in the *Jewish Encyclopedia*, vol. 16 (Kelen Publishing House, 1971). This knowledge lay dormant for several years until my father was diagnosed with a terminal illness in 1990. I began to appreciate the importance of this custom as I became more involved in hospice care and saw the spiritual suffering experienced by some of our patients.

The work of James O. Prochaska, Ph.D., and Carlo DiClemente, Ph.D., and the development in 1979 of their *Transtheoretical Model/Stages of Change,* inspired the six stages of readiness described in this chapter. The model has been applied in the assessment and treatment of addiction problems (adapted from W. R. Miller and S. Rollnick's *Motivational Interviewing: Preparing People to Change Addictive Behavior* [Guilford Press, 1991]).

More recently, this model has been adapted for use in many areas where the assessment of readiness for a behavior change is useful, most notably in health education and health promotion. I was introduced to the use of this model for diet, exercise, and tobacco cessation efforts through the HealthPartners Center for Health Promotion, Bloomington, Minnesota.

CHAPTER TWO

The idea for the quotation from *Hamlet* was obtained from an article on ethical wills written by Jerome Apfel, in the *Pennsylvania Bar Association Quarterly,* vol. XLIX (January 1978). I would never have been able to unearth this treasure without the help of Dennis Geller, a supporter and fellow proponent of this custom.

The Judaic roots of ethical wills provide for many examples in the Hebrew Bible. My friend and Rabbi, Harold Kravitz, and another acquaintance, Rabbi Esther Adler-Rephan, pointed out the citations.

The tradition of ethical wills has threads throughout the Christian Bible as well. Numerous citations were pointed out to me by Phil Boe, MDiv and hospice chaplain for Hospice of the Lakes, Bloomington, Minnesota, and Jerry Casterton, R.N., a coworker and hospice nurse at Hospice of the Lakes.

Other historical references on ethical wills come from the *Jewish Encyclopedia*. The prototypical medieval ethical will is that of Judah ibn Tibbon, written in the late twelfth century.

Elyse Rabinowitz, an active member of Hadassah in Minneapolis, graciously shared her information sources on women's ethical wills of the Renaissance period. The most notable is *The Memoirs of Glukel of Hameln,* written in the 1690s.

A local Minneapolis attorney and acquaintance, Peter Lennington, brought issues about the legal status of ethical wills to my attention.

The ethical will themes were derived from a number of ethical wills primarily contained in Riemer and Stampfer's *So That Your Values Live On*. Reading through their collection of ethical wills from the early 1800s through the late 1970s provided an excellent grounding in common ethical will themes.

CHAPTER THREE

The main source of information for this chapter came from the many ethical wills workshops I've presented, and the openness of the participants to share their stories and feelings of highly personal events in their lives. Previously referenced books and articles also provided some insight and reasons for why people choose to write an ethical will.

Several individuals who shared their stories that became "universal" examples of how challenging life events and transitional stages in life can propel someone to create an ethical will: Elaine Ellis-Stone, who tapped into the deep meaning of her first pregnancy to write her ethical will; Judy, who faced the unknown outcome of upcoming brain surgery to write her "what if" letters to her children; Jennifer Isham, who has worked with noncustodial parents of divorce and has integrated the use of ethical wills as a healing tool.

Chapter Four

A special note of thanks to the Hospice of the Lakes volunteers who participated in training to become "ethical will coaches." They allowed me the flexibility to experiment with and perfect the first approach for writing an ethical will. Their feedback and experience with this exercise were invaluable for its development.

Phil Boe, MDiv, a chaplain for Hospice of the Lakes, worked closely with me to develop some initial exercises he could use with patients to quickly put together an ethical will, particularly exercises #1, #2, and #3. His interest and enthusiasm were major ingredients for the successful application of ethical wills in hospice and palliative care. He was always willing to try out different ideas and his feedback from his work with our hospice patients was incredibly helpful for creating useful exercises for this book's second approach to writing an ethical will.

There were helpful ideas for exercises #4 and #5 generated from Riemer and Stampfer's *So That Your Values Live On*.

I was introduced to the concept pertaining to exercises #6 and #7 from several sources. My first exposure to these suggestions as guided writing exercises occurred while attending the Covey Leadership Training Program in 1988. In *From Age-ing to Sage-ing*, by Zalman Shacter-Shalomi and Ronald Miller (New York: Warner Books, 1997), these concepts are also presented. Finally, my good friend and colleague Rachael Freed has experimented with adaptations of this material for exercises in her spiritual-ethical will seminars. She learned of similar material from Natalie Goldberg's *Wild Mind: Living the Writer's Life* (New York: Bantam, 1990).

Sara Burstein provided much of the structural ideas for the common journaling techniques section for approach #3. *So That Your Values Live On* and my own personal experiences with workshop training provided the core content for how best to organize information for writing an ethical will.

CHAPTER FIVE

All of the authors of the ethical wills contained in Appendix 1 taught me many lessons on how to share an ethical will. My spouse, Sandy, provided a process for preservation of ethical wills by designing an archival keepsake folder and hand-painted paper as tangible examples of how this can be accomplished.

The cautions and unethical uses of ethical wills are amply illustrated in the Hebrew Bible (Genesis, chapter 49). I also used an excerpt from an ethical will previously published in *So That Your Values Live On*.

CHAPTER 6

The articles that provided the survival statistics for CPR are as follows: Ian Jacobs et al., "The Chain of Survival," *Annals of Emergency Medicine* 37, no. 4 (April 2001): S5–S16; and Bruce D. Adams et al., "Emergency Medicine Residents Effectively Direct Inhospital Cardiac Arrest Teams," *American Journal of Emergency Medicine* 23, no. 3 (May 2005): 304–310.

The American Medical Association's "Education for Physicians on End of Life Care" program provided an excellent database on living will information. I completed the association's train-the-trainer program a number of years ago.

Many of my palliative care colleagues offered their suggestions on the technical content of the chapter.

ACKNOWLEDGMENTS

Where do I begin?

More than anything else, I feel blessed for having the opportunity to synthesize the learnings and experiences I have had over the past ten years. The culmination of which has been the creation of this book.

I owe thanks to many people—both known and unknown to me. My journey with ethical wills has deeply affected my own spiritual dimension and heightened my awareness and appreciation of this aspect of all individuals.

First, thanks to my dad, Norman, who died in 1990 of cancer. He was quite courageous in taking the step of writing that "letter" to me before he died. To my mom, Anne, for helping Dad put his values on paper. I wish you had had time to do the same.

It's unlikely that this book would ever have been written if I hadn't become involved with end-of-life care. For that, I owe a debt of gratitude to the staff at HealthPartners Hospice of the Lakes, Minneapolis, Minnesota. In particular, to Phil Boe, MDiv, our hospice chaplain who nurtured the idea of using ethical wills in hospice care, and who challenged me to create resources to enable patients to make an ethical will easily and quickly when urgency was high and time was short.

A special thanks to my wife, Sandy, for being patient with me, and for her support and help on this project. Thanks to my daughters, Alisha and Hannah, for providing purpose and meaning to my life. Whether they know it or not, they were a significant motivating force behind this effort.

Thank you to Ilana Favero, Mike Favero, Barb Friedman, Lon Rosenfield, Jerry Rosen, and Martha Brand (members of my running group, "the Windbreakers") for listening to my chatter about ethical wills over the past four years. I want to single out Lon for special thanks for his guidance and listening as we ran around Lake of the Isles.

To David Alme, thank you for always being there when I needed to process some tough issues.

I appreciate the support of my Legacy Center colleagues, Doug Baker, Rachael Freed, Bev Lutz, Dan Taylor, and Mary O'Brien Tyrrell. They helped me broaden my perspective of what a legacy entails.

In reviewing my initial chapters, thanks goes to Sandy Baines, Isidore Berenbaum, Bonnie Dudovitz, Ardyce Ehrlich, Linda Norlander, Kate Sandweiss, and Dan Tobin.

Thanks to Sara Burstein for her editorial advice, suggestions, and efforts on restructuring the manuscript.

Many thanks to Rachael Freed, a fellow cofounder of the Legacy Center and an author in her own right, for providing me with the most significant insights and suggestions for improving the manuscript and helping this book to reach a new level.

Thank you to my friend Dan Tobin, who has provided unwavering support and encouragement for this book from the very beginning. Without his help, who knows what the fate of this book would have been.

Thanks to Marnie Cochran, Executive Editor at Da Capo Press, for believing in the value of sharing this work with as wide an audience as possible.

Finally, thanks to all of the courageous souls who shared their ethical wills with me. Your legacies will live on.

Forgive me for any omissions in my acknowledgments; I have a great memory, it's just too short!

Acknowledgments for the Second Edition of Ethical Wills

First, I want to acknowledge my friend and colleague, C. J. Peek, for his help on the first edition.

Second, thank you, Marnie Cochran, for your delicate approach and great idea to have me add a chapter on living wills to the second edition of *Ethical Wills*.

Third, thank you, Sandy, for your ongoing support of my ethical will journey and your input.

Finally, I want to thank Bonnie, Rachael, Lon, Paul, Neil, Kate, Jerry, Marty, Keith, and Linda. I was delighted with the synergy and diversity of your thoughtful and candid comments on the living wills chapter. You all played an important role in the development of the second edition.